GHALIB

Persian Poems

For a list and descriptions of our over 700 titles
go to amazon.com/author/smithpa

GHALIB
Persian Poems

Translation and Introduction

Paul Smith

New Humanity Books
Book Heaven
Booksellers & Publishers

New Humanity Books

BOOK HEAVEN

(Booksellers & Publishers for 40 years)

47 Main Road Campbells Creek

Victoria Australia

amazon.com/author/smithpa

ISBN ISBN: 978-1545495728

Poetry/Sufism/ Persian Poetry, Sufi Poetry

Indian Literature/ History/Mysticism/Ghalib

CONTENTS

Ghalib's tomb, Delhi.

Ghalib: His Life, Times and Poetry

Mirza Ghalib was born Mirza Asadullah Baig Khan, (born on 27 December 1797 – died 15 February 1869), was a classical Urdu and Persian poet from the Mughal Empire during British colonial rule. He used his pen-names of Ghalib meaning 'dominant' and Asad meaning 'lion'. During his lifetime the Mughals were eclipsed and displaced by the British and finally deposed following the defeat of the Indian rebellion of 1857, events that he wrote about. Most notably, he wrote some 500 *ghazals* in Urdu and Persian during his life that have since been interpreted and sung in many different ways by different people. Ghalib, the last great poet of the Mughal Era, is considered to be one of the most popular and influential poets of the Urdu language. Ghalib today remains popular not only in India and Pakistan but also among their communities scattered around the world.

Mirza Ghalib was born in Agra into a family descended from Aibak Turks who moved to Samarkand (now in Uzbekistan) after the downfall of the Seljuk kings. His paternal grandfather, Mirza Qoqan Baig Khan, was a Saljuq Turk who had immigrated to India from Samarkand during the reign of Ahmad

Shah (1748–54). He worked at Lahore, Delhi and Jaipur, was awarded the sub-district of Pahasu (Bulandshahr, U.P.) and finally settled in Agra, U.P., India. He had four sons and three daughters. Mirza Abdullah Baig Khan and Mirza Nasrullah Baig Khan were two of his sons. Mirza Abdullah Baig Khan (Ghalib's father) was married to Izzat-ut-Nisa Begum and then lived at the house of his father- in-law. He was employed first by the Nawab of Lucknow and then the Nizam of Hyderabad, Deccan. He died in a battle in 1803 in Alwar and was buried at Rajgarh (Alwar, Rajasthan). At the time Ghalib was a little over 5 years of age. He was raised at first by his Uncle Mirza Nasrullah Baig Khan who started taking care of the three orphaned children. He was the governor of Agra under the Marathas. The British appointed him an officer of 400 cavalrymen, fixed his salary at Rs.1700.00 month, and awarded him 2 *parganas* (one or more villages and the surrounding countryside) in Mathura (U.P.). When he died in 1806, the British took away the *parganas* and fixed his pension as Rs. 10,000 per year, linked to the state of Firozepur Jhirka (Mewat, Haryana). The Nawab of Ferozepur Jhirka reduced the pension to Rs. 3000 per year. Ghalib's share was Rs. 62.50 per month.

Ghalib married Umrao Begum, daughter of Nawab Ilahi Bakhsh (brother of the Nawab of Ferozepur Jhirka). He soon moved to Delhi, along with his younger brother, Mirza Yousuf Khan, who had developed schizophrenia at a young age and later died in Delhi during the chaos of 1857. In accordance with upper class Muslim tradition Ghalib's was an arranged marriage at the age of 13, but none of his seven children survived beyond infancy. In one of his letters he describes his marriage as the second imprisonment after the initial confinement that was life itself. The idea that life is one continuous painful struggle which can end only when life itself ends is a recurring theme in his poetry.

In 1850, Emperor Bahadur Shah Zafar II (also a poet of Persian *ghazals* *(see selected Bibliography)*... bestowed upon Mirza Ghalib a number of titles. The conferment of these titles was symbolic of Mirza Ghalib's incorporation into the nobility of Delhi. He was also an important courtier of the royal court of the Emperor. As the Emperor was himself a poet, Mirza Ghalib was appointed as his poet tutor in 1854. He was also appointed as tutor of Prince Fakhr-ud Din Mirza, eldest son of Bahadur Shah II, (d. 10 July 1856). He was also appointed by the Emperor as the royal historian of Mughal Court. Being a member of declining Mughal nobility and old landed aristocracy, he never worked for a livelihood, living on either royal patronage of Mughal Emperors, credit or the generosity of his friends. His fame came to him posthumously. He had himself remarked during his lifetime that he would be recognized by later generations. After the decline of the Mughal Empire and the rise of the British Raj, despite his many attempts, Ghalib could never get the full pension restored.

Ghalib started composing poetry at the age of 11. His first language was Urdu, but Persian and Turkish were also spoken at home. He received an education in Persian and Arabic at a young age. When Ghalib was in his early teens, a newly converted Muslim tourist from Iran (Abdus Samad, originally named Hormuzd, a Zoroastrian) came to Agra. He stayed at Ghalib's home for two years and taught him Persian, Arabic, philosophy, and logic.

Although Ghalib himself was far prouder of his poetic achievements in Persian, he is today more famous for his Urdu *ghazals*. In keeping with the conventions of the classical Persian *ghazal, ruba'i, qit'a* and *masnavi*, in most of Ghalib's verses, the identity and the gender of the beloved is indeterminate. The convention of having the 'idea' of a lover or beloved instead of an actual lover/beloved freed the poet-protagonist-lover from the demands of realism.

Dr. Arifshah Gilani, author of 'Ghalib: His Life and Persian Poetry' (see bibliography) states: "Ghalib *is,* to all intents and purposes, the last of the great classical poets of the Indo-Pakistan sub-continent, because although the late Dr. Sir Muhammad Iqbal has made a distinct and valuable contribution in Persian poetry, still in so far as the *language* is concerned, he cannot be said to have even approached Ghalib, much less surpassed him."

He also states, "Strictly speaking, the real Ghalib lies not only in the twelve hundred Urdu verses but also in the twelve thousand and odd couplets of his Persian poetry... Like an eagle he flew over all the rest. In fact, he was a giant amongst the pygmies. His many sided genius should earn him and abiding niche in the domain of Persian poetry."

And, Nazir Ahmad in his Introduction to Dr. Yusuf Hussain's 'Persian *Ghazals* of Ghalib' (see bibliography) states: "Ghalib's Persian *ghazals* have great ethical value. According to him man is the best of creation; he should not debase himself at any cost; he should not accept gratification which results in self-mortification... Ghalib was not a mystic; but his poetry specially his *ghazals* are full of mystical thought. It is to be noted that in the treatment of mystical ideas he has given new and original interpretations."

Numerous elucidations of Ghalib's *ghazal* compilations have been written by Urdu scholars. The first such elucidation or

Sharh was written by Ali Haider Nazm Tabatabai of Hyderabad during the rule of the last Nizam of Hyderabad. Before Ghalib, the Urdu *ghazal* was primarily an expression of anguished love; but Ghalib expressed philosophy, the travails and mysteries of life and wrote *ghazals* on many other subjects, vastly expanding the scope of the *ghazal*. This work is considered to be his paramount contribution to Urdu poetry and literature.

Love poetry in Urdu from the last quarter of the seventeenth century onwards consists mostly of 'poems about love' and not 'love poems' in the Western sense of the term.

Mirza Ghalib was a gifted letter writer. Not only Urdu poetry but the prose is also indebted to Mirza Ghalib. His letters gave foundation to easy and popular Urdu. Before Ghalib, letter writing in Urdu was highly ornamental. He made his letters 'talk' by using words and sentences as if he were conversing with the reader. According to him *Sau kos se ba-zaban-e-qalam baatein kiya karo aur hijr mein visaal ke maze liya karo* (from hundred of miles talk with the tongue of the pen and enjoy the joy of meeting even when you are separated). His letters were very informal, some times he would just write the name of the person and start the letter. He was very humorous and wrote very interesting letters. In one letter he wrote "Main koshish karta hoon keh koi aesi baat likhoon jo parhay khoosh ho jaaye" (I want to write lines such that whoever reads them would enjoy them). Some scholar says that Ghalib would have the same place in Urdu literature if only on the basis of his letters. They have been translated into English by Ralph Russell, see *'The Oxford Ghalib'* (see Selected Bibliography following).

Ghalib was a chronicler of a turbulent period. One by one, Ghalib saw the bazaars – Khas Bazaar, Urdu Bazaar, Kharam-ka Bazaar, disappear, whole *mohallas* (localities) and *katras* (lanes) vanish. The *havelis* (mansions) of his friends were razed to the ground. Ghalib wrote that Delhi had become a desert. Water was scarce. Delhi was now 'a military camp'. It was the end of the feudal elite to which Ghalib had belonged.

Ghalib was proud of his reputation as a rake. He was once imprisoned for gambling and subsequently relished the affair with pride. In the Mughal court circles he even acquired a reputation as a 'ladies' man'.

He was a very liberal mystic who believed that "the search for God within liberated the seeker from the narrowly Orthodox Islam, encouraging the devotee to look beyond the letter of the law to its narrow essence."

His Sufi views and mysticism is reflected in many of his

poems and *ghazals*. Like many other Urdu poets, Ghalib was capable of writing profoundly religious poetry, yet was skeptical about the literalist interpretation of the Islamic scriptures. Like Hafiz he staunchly disdained the Orthodox Muslim Sheikhs of the Ulema, who in his poems always represent narrow-mindedness and hypocrisy. He criticized them for their ignorance and arrogant certitude: "Look deeper, it is you alone who cannot hear the music of his secrets".

In his letters, Ghalib frequently contrasted the narrow legalism of the Ulema with its pre-occupation with its narrow teaching and real spirituality for which you had to "study the works of the mystics and take into one's heart the essential truth of God's reality and his expression in all things".

Ghalib believed that if God laid within and could be reached less by ritual than by love, then he was as accessible to Hindus as to Muslims. As a testament to this, he would later playfully write in a letter that during a trip to Benares, he was half tempted to settle down there for good and that he wished he had renounced Islam, put a Hindu sectarian mark on his forehead, tied a sectarian thread around his waist and seated himself on the banks of the Ganges so that he could wash the contamination of his existence away from himself and like a drop be one with the river.

During the anti-British Rebellion in Delhi on 5 October 1857, three weeks after the British troops had entered through Kashmiri Gate, some soldiers went into Ghalib's neighbourhood and hauled him off to Colonel Burn for questioning. He appeared in front of the colonel wearing a Central Asian Turkic style headdress. The colonel, bemused at his appearance, inquired in broken Urdu, "Well? You Muslim?" To which Ghalib replied, "Half!" The colonel asked, "What does that mean?" In response, Ghalib said, "I drink wine, but I don't eat pork."

Ghalib's closest rival was poet Zauq, tutor of Bahadur Shah Zafar II, the then emperor of India with his seat in Delhi. There are some amusing anecdotes of the competition between Ghalib and Zauq and exchange of jibes between them. However, there was mutual respect for each other's talent. Both also admired and acknowledged the supremacy of Mir, a towering figure of 18th century Urdu Poetry. Another poet Momin, whose *ghazals* had a distinctly lyrical flavour, was also a famous contemporary of Ghalib. Ghalib was not only a poet, he was also a prolific prose writer. His letters are a reflection of the political and social climate of the time. They also refer to many contemporaries like Mir Mehdi Majrooh, who himself was a good poet and Ghalib's lifelong acquaintance. See my

'*Shimmering Jewels: Anthology Under the Reigns of the Mughal Poets of India (1526-1857)*' pages 411-461 for the poets of his time including Zauq, Momin and Zafar.

Indian Cinema has paid a tribute to the legendary poet through a film (in sepia/black and white) named *Mirza Ghalib* (1954) in which Bharat Bhushan plays Ghalib and Suraiya plays his courtesan lover, Chaudvin. The musical score of the film was composed by Ghulam Mohammed and his compositions of Ghalib's famous *ghazals* are likely to remain everlasting favorites.

Pakistani Cinema has also paid tribute to the legendary poet through another film also named *Mirza Ghalib*. The film was directed by M.M. Billoo Mehra and produced as well by M.M. Billoo Mehra for S.K. Pictures. The music was composed by Tassaduq Hussain. The film starred Pakistani film superstar *Sudhir* playing Ghalib and Madam Noor Jehan playing his courtesan lover, Chaudvin. The film was released on 24 November 1961 and reached average status at the box-office, however, the music remains memorable in Pakistan to this day.

Gulzar produced a TV serial, *Mirza Ghalib* (1988), telecast on DD National that was immensely successful in India. Naseeruddin Shah played the role of Ghalib in the serial, and it featured *ghazals* sung and composed by Jagjit Singh and Chitra

Singh. Serial's music has since been recognized as Jagjit Singh and Chitra Singh's magnum opus enjoying a cult following in the Indian subcontinent. The serial was colored by contemporary Indian nationalism, and Ghalib's persona was frequently a vehicle for propaganda in favour of national unity.

The Pakistan government in 1969 commissioned Khaliq Ibrahim (died 2006) to make a documentary on Mirza Ghalib. The movie was completed in 1971-72. It is said, that the movie, a docudrama, was historically more correct than what the official Pakistan government point of view was. Thus, it was never released. Till this date, barring a few private viewing, the movie is lying with the Department of Films and Publication, Government of Pakistan. The movie was made on 16 mm format. Ghalib's role was played by actor Subhani Bayunus, who later played this role in many TV productions.

Ghalib must be the only Poet who had biggest number of Stage portrayals. Various Theatre groups have traditionally staged plays related to the life of Mirza Ghalib. These have shown different lifestyles and the way he lived his life. Starting from the Parsi Theatre and Hindustani Theatre days the first phase of his Stage Portrayal culminated in Sheila Bhatia's Production which was written by Mehdi Saheb. Mohd Ayub performed his role so many times that many theatre goers used to know him as Ghalib. Sheila Bhatia Production was basically celebration of his famous *ghazals* that used to be presented one after another. Ghalib's character lacked required nuances and was shown philandering with the courtesan played famously by Punjabi singer Madan Bala Sandhu. Later Begum Abida Ahmed wife of late President Fakhruddin Ali Ahmed supported many very costly productions. This was perhaps the golden period of Ghalib productions as many other productions also were done including Surender Verma's Play which was done by National School of Drama. *Qaid-e-Hayat* (Imprisonment of Life, 1983) written by Surendra Verma talks about the personal life of poet Ghalib, including his financial hardships and his tragic love for Katiba, a woman calligraphist, who was working on his *diwan*. Over the years, it has been directed by numerous theatre directors, including Ram Gopal Bajaj in 1989, at the National School of Drama. This period also saw numerous College and University Productions done by Student Groups. The writers whose scripts were more popular during this period were Jameel Shaidai, Danish Iqbal, Devender Singh and few others. In recent years Dr Sayeed Alam's 'Ghalib in New Delhi' started another phase with contempoarary fun & frolic. Sayeed Alam has had more than 250 shows around the world. Danish Iqbal's Play 'Ghalib-e Khasta ke Baghair' was staged in Aurangabad, Aligarh and at few other places on the occasion of 150th year of India's first war of Independence. Sayeed Alam also wrote a non-comic version of 'Ghalib' played by veteran actor Tom Alter; this play is also a well known Production which is frequently staged... and written by Dr. Sayeed Alam was staged many times in Delhi.

Another Play 'Main Gaya Waqt Nahin Hoon' written by Danish Iqbal, provides a fresh spin to the never ending spin to the character of Ghalib. Sayeed Alam's new production is inspired from the famous letters of Ghalib. An animation film on Mirza Ghalib was telecast on Zee Cinema.

Gulzar's
Mirza Ghalib

Complete collection featuring unreleased Ghazals, Couplets & Dialogues in the
JAGJIT SINGH, NASEERUDDIN SHAH & Others.

Selected Bibliography

The Book of Ghalib: Translation & Introduction by Paul Smith, New Humanity Books Campbells Creek, 2014.

Ghalib: Life & Poems, Translation & Introduction by Paul Smith, New Humanity Books Campbells Creek, 2015.

Ghalib: Selected Poems, Translation & Introduction by Paul Smith, New Humanity Books, Campbells Creek, 2012.

Persian Ghazals of Ghalib, Translated into English by Dr. Yusuf Husain Khan, Ghalib Institute, New Delhi, 1980. (Most are qit'as, not ghazals).

Selections from the Persian Ghazals of Ghalib with Translations into English by Ralph & Urdu by Iftikhar Ahmad Adani, Pakistan Writers' Co-operative Society, Pakistan, 1997.

Ghazals of Ghalib, Ouijas Ahmad Editor... Columbia University Press, New York, 1971.

Persian Poetry of Mirza Ghalib: Translated with an Introduction by Shafi Shaq, Pen Productions, Shrinagar, 2000.

Bahadur Shah Zafar: Sufi Poet & Last Mughal Emperor & His Circle of Poets... Zauq, Ghalib, Momin, Shefta, Dagh ~Selected Poems~ Translation & Introduction by Paul Smith, New Humanity Books Campbells Creek, 2017.

Wikipedia article on Ghalib.

Divan-e-Ghalib; Complete Translation into English, Including All the Ghazals, Qasidas, Masnavis, Qitas & Quatrains of the Published Divan and A selection from the unpublished Divan, Translated by Saruta Raman. Ghalib Institute, New Delhi, 2003. (Urdu poems only)

Ghalib: His Life and Persian Poetry by Dr. Arifshah C. Sayyid Gilani, Azam Book Corporation, Karachi, 1962 2nd ed.

The Aesthetics of Appropriation: Ghalib's Persian Ghazal Poetry and its Critics by Gregory Maxwell Bruce, University of Texas, Austin, 2012.

The Oxford India Ghalib, Edited by Ralph Russell, O.U.P. New Delhi, 2007. (Contains trans. of some of his Persian poems).

Love Sonnets of Ghalib, Translated by Sarfaraz. K. Niazi, Rupa & Co., New Delhi. 2002.

The *Ghazal* in Persian Poetry

There is really no equivalent to the *ghazal* (pronounced *guz'el*) in English poetry... although as Masud Farzaad, the greatest Iranian authority on Hafiz and his *ghazals* said, the sonnet is probably the closest. As a matter of fact, the *ghazal* is a unique form and its origin has been argued about for many centuries.

Some say that the *ghazal* originated in songs that were composed in Persia to be sung at court before Persia was converted to Islam, but not one song has survived to prove this. It is also possible that originally the *ghazals* were songs of love that were sung by minstrels in the early days of Persian history and that this form passed into poetry down the ages. I find this explanation plausible for the following reasons: firstly, the word *ghazal* means (among other things) 'a conversation between lovers'. Secondly, the Persian *ghazals* of Hafiz, Sadi, Ghalib and others were often put to music and became songs, which have been popular in Persia and the Indian Sub-continent from ancient times until now.

Other scholars see the *ghazal* as coming from Arabic poetry, especially the prelude to longer poems, i.e. the *qasida:* they say that this prelude was isolated and changed, to eventually become the *ghazal*. The Arabic root of the word *ghazal* is *gazl* which means: spinning, spun, thread, twist… the form of the *ghazal* is a spiral. Whatever the origin, by the fourteenth century the *ghazal* had become a mature form of poetry. Among the great *ghazal* writers in Persian of the past were Nizami, 'Attar, Rumi, and Sadi and in Turkish, Yunus Emre; but with the *ghazals* of Hafiz and other poets in Shiraz during his lifetime, this form reached its summit… most other poets of the *ghazal*, whether in Persian, Turkish, Urdu, Pushtu, English or any other language were influenced by his *ghazals*.

The form of the *ghazal* at first glance seems simple, but on a deeper inspection it will be found that there is more to it than one at first sees. It is usually between five and fifteen couplets *(beyts* or 'houses'), but sometimes more. A *beyt* is 'a line of verse split into two equal parts scanning exactly alike.' Each couplet has a fixed rhyme which appears at the end of the second line. In the first couplet which is called the *matla* meaning 'orient' or 'rising,' the rhyme appears at the end of both lines. This first couplet has the function of 'setting the stage' or stating the subject matter and feeling of the poem. The other couplets or *beyts* have other names depending on their positions. One could say that the opening couplet is the subject, the following couplets the actions: changing, viewed from different angles, progressing from one point to another, larger and deeper, until the objective of the poem is reached in the last couplet. The final couplet is known as the *maqta* or 'point of section.' This couplet or the one before it, almost always contains the *takhallus* or pen-name of the poet, signifying that it was written by him and also allowing him the chance to detach himself from himself and comment on what effect the actions of the subject matter in the preceding couplets had on him. Often the poet uses a play on words when he uses his own pen-name... ('Hafiz' for example, means: a preserver, a guardian, rememberer, watchman, one who knows the *Koran* by heart. 'Ghalib' means: victorious).

In the *ghazal* the Arabic, Persian, Turkish, Urdu and Pushtu poets found the ideal instrument to express the great tension between the opposites that exist in this world. Having the strict rhyming structure of the same rhyme at the end of the second line of each couplet (after the first couplet) the mind must continually come back to the world and the poem and the rhyme. But by being allowed to use any word at the end of the first line of each couplet, one can be as spontaneous as possible and give the heart its full rein. This of course happens also in the first line of the first couplet, for whatever word or rhyme-sound that comes out in the first line sets the rhyme for the rest of the *ghazal*. So the 'feeling' created by the rhyme is one that comes spontaneously from the heart, and this spontaneity is allowed to be expanded from then on in the non-rhyming lines, and to contract in those lines that rhyme, when the mind must function as an 'orderer' of the poem. This expansion and contraction, feeling and thinking, heart and mind, combine to produce great tension and power that spirals inward and outward and creates an atmosphere that I would define as 'deep nostalgia.' This deep nostalgia is a primal moving force that flows through all life, art and song, and produces within whoever comes into contact with it when it is consciously expressed, an irresistible yearning to unite the opposites that it contains. In the *ghazal* any metre can be employed except the *ruba'i* metre.

The true meaning of Sufism, apart from the recognition of God in human form as the *Qutub* or the *Rasool* or the Christ is *tassawuf...* which means to get to the essence of everything. Adam was the first poet and it is said that he named everything and invented the first alphabet from which all others come. But Adam was not only the creator of conscious language as we know it, he was also the creator of song and the perfect form through which he created songs in praise of Eve his true Beloved, her beauty was displayed in the spiral form of the *ghazal*. So, the *ghazals* he composed and sung to her before their eventual Spiritual Union were of longing and separation and those after... of the bliss of Union. He used the same form of song about other events including the great sorrow and deep nostalgia about the loss of his favourite son Abel.

Two of Arabia's most careful and serious historians Tabari (d.923) and Masudi (d.957) state that the first poem ever composed in known history was one by Adam (the original Sufi *Qutub* or First Perfect Master... God-man) on the death of Abel and the form was the *ghazal*...

The lands are changed and all those who live upon them,

the face of the earth is torn and surrounded with gloom;

everything that was lovely and fragrant has now faded,

from that beautiful face has vanished the joyful bloom.

What deep regrets for my dear son... O regrets for Abel,

a victim of murder... who has been placed into the tomb!

Is it possible to rest, while that Devil that was cursed

who never fails or dies... up from behind us does loom?

"Give up these lands and all of those who live on them;

I was the one who forced you out of Paradise, your room,

where you and your wife were so secure and established,

where your heart did not know of the world's dark doom!

But you, you did escape all of my traps and my trickery,

until that great gift of life... upon which you did presume

you went and lost... and from Aden the blasts of wind,

but for God's Grace would've swept you, like a broom."

It is said that thousands of years after Adam, the Perfect Spiritual Master Noah, settled Shiraz after his ark landed in the Turkish lands on the mountains of Ararat and was a vintner who brought the first vines that he carried with him was also a poet who composed in this form as did the *Qutub* of some three thousand years later who also settled his people he had led from their homeland in Bactria (northern Afghanistan) to Fars (Persia)... Zoroaster.

His *gathas* or hymns are in rhyme-structure the first two couplets of the *ghazal* which would later be known as the *ruba'i*. And so the *ghazals* of the Zoroastrians were sung in their winehouses and fire temples throughout our land until the Muslim Arabs invaded and converted most to Islam, but poets and minstrels would not give up their much loved eternal God-given *ghazal* or the wine of Noah as well, which had its distant progeny in the *mesqali* grape.

The clandestine winehouses run by the Zoroastrians and Christians became the venues for many hundreds of years of the *ghazal*. In these winehouses Persians could criticise their Arab and Turkish rulers and their police chiefs and false Sufi masters and hypocritical clergy who censored and forbade them to practice the drinking of wine and the appreciation of beautiful faces and forms of unveiled women and handsome young men.

In the winehouses the truth could be told and this truth was quickly spread by the minstrels in the market places and even at court through what was becoming a popular form of expression amongst the masses. And although in fact the actual drinking of wine finally became less because of the religious restrictions, it as a symbol of truth, love and freedom became more widespread.

Of course there always existed another 'Winehouse' where the Wine of Divine Love and Grace was poured out by the Winebringer or *Qutub,* the Perfect Master or the Old Magian. Here the wine and truth that flowed freely from heart to heart was of the spiritual nature and made the lover or drunkard so intoxicated with the Divine Beloved that he became *mast-like*... mad with longing to be united with the Eternal One, Whose beauty he saw and appreciated in the face and form and personality of his earthly beloved whom he praised, wooed, begged, cajoled, described, desired and desperately longed for through his *ghazals* and by his actions and with each breath of his whole life he came closer to the Eternal Beloved. Human love became transmuted into Divine Love. Hafiz's love for Shakh-e Nabat and Ibn 'Arabi's for Nizam are an examples of this.

Although the poets of the *ghazal* may appear to many as open-minded, drunken, outcast lovers, it does not necessarily mean that they all drank the juice of the grape... for it is an inner state that they often were expressing. The *ghazal* is usually a conversation between the lover and the beloved and as in all intimate conversation... the talk flows both ways. The subject may not necessary be about love, but it is always from the point of view of one who loves truth, love and beauty.

The *ghazal* not only has a specific form, but traditionally deals with just one subject: Love. And not any kind of love, but specifically, an illicit, and unattainable love. The subcontinental *ghazals* have an influence of Sufism and the subject of love can usually be interpreted for a higher being or for a mortal beloved. The love is always viewed as something that will complete a human being, and if attained will lift him or her into the ranks of the wise, or will bring satisfaction to the soul of the poet. Traditional *ghazal* love may or may not have an explicit element of sexual desire in it, and hence the love may be spiritual. The *ghazal* is nearly always written from the point of view of the unrequited lover, whose beloved is portrayed as unattainable.

Most often either the beloved does not return the poet's love or returns it without sincerity, or else the societal circumstances do not allow it. The lover is aware and resigned to this fate but continues loving nonetheless; the lyrical impetus of the poem derives from this tension. Representations of the lover's powerlessness to resist his feelings often include lyrically exaggerated violence. It is not possible to get a full understanding of *ghazal* poetry without at least being familiar with some concepts of Sufism. Many of the major historical post-Islamic *ghazal* poets were either avowed Sufis themselves or were sympathizers with Sufi ideas. Most *ghazals* can be viewed in a spiritual context, with the Beloved being a metaphor for God, or the poet's spiritual master. It is the intense Divine Love of Sufism that serves as a model for most of the forms of love found in *ghazal* poetry.

Most *ghazal* scholars today recognize that some *ghazal* couplets are exclusively about Divine Love, others are about 'earthly love', but many of them can be interpreted in either context. In keeping with the conventions of the *ghazal* and other forms in Urdu and Persian poetry, in most poems the identity and the gender of the beloved is indeterminate, both languages having no 'he' or 'she'. The beloved could be a beautiful woman, boy, man, monarch, or God or the Perfect Master as in Sufi poetry. I usually translate this as 'you' or 'that one', although most translators over the centuries of Persian and Urdu fall into the trap of designating a particular sex.

Sources…

Literary History of Persia Volume 2 by E.G. Browne. Cambridge University Press, 1928. (Pages 22-76).

History of Iranian Literature by Jan Rupka et al. D. Reidel Publishing Company, Dordrecht. 1968. (pages 91-105).

Classical Persian Literature by A.J. Arberry. George Allen & Unwin Ltd. London. 1958. (Pages 1-16).

Masterpieces of Urdu Ghazals: From the 17th to the 20th Century by K.C. Kanda, Sterling Publishers pvt Ltd, New Delhi 1992. (Pages 1-15).

A History of Ottoman Poetry by E.J.W. Gibb Volume One Luzac and Company. London, 1958. (pages 70-83).

Ghazal as World Literature 1: Transformations of a Literary Genre, Edited by Thomas Bauer and Angelika Neuwith, Orient-Institut, Beriut, 2005.

The *Ruba'i* in Persian Poetry

Many scholars of Persian Poetry believe that the *ruba'i* is the most ancient Persian poetic form that is original to this language and they state that all other classical forms including the *ghazal, qasida, masnavi, qit'a* and others originated in Arabic literature and the metres employed in them were in Arabic poetry in the beginning... this, can be disputed.

The Persian language is a fine intercourse of Arabic (a masculine-sounding language) and Pahlavi (feminine-sounding language) which is mainly a descendant of the profound language of the Spiritual Master Zoroaster... Zend. Sanskrit is also a branch of that ancient language* (e.g. Zend: *garema* or heat is in Sanskrit *gharma,* in Pahlavi is *garma,* Persian... *garm*) given to us by that prophet whose perfect and profound teachings in the *gathas* of the *Avesta* were composed in a form very close to the *ruba'i* which one might believe could give him the title not only of the founder of the Persian language and people and mysticism... but also of Persian poetry's most individualistic form of poetic expression.

One can trace the origins of this poetical language back almost 7000 years to Zoroaster's time, not merely less than

2600 years... a mistake that most recent scholars made by confusing the last Zoroastian *priest* bearing his name with that of this original Prophet, the *Rasool* or Messiah, who like Moses, led out his people from their original Arayan lands in Bactria, when they were invaded by many hordes of murderous barbarians.

On that remarkable and in many aspects, far-reaching journey, an argument occurred amongst his people when they had reached what we today call India and many left him and settled there and their language eventually evolved into Sanskrit. Zoroaster then took his remaining followers west and finally settled near Shiraz in Fars, and Zend eventually became Pahlavi and the Arayan language continued west and founded many languages in Europe, including English.

Now as to the origin of the metre of the *ruba'i* I offer two of Zoroaster's poems or *gathas* to enjoy and consider, even though the metre may not be that of the *ruba'i,* the rhyme structure and content are similar.

Wise One, with these short poems I come before You,
praising Your Righteousness, deeds of Good Mind too.
And when I arrive at that bliss that has come to me...
may these poems of this man of insight... come through.
And another...

May good rulers and not evil ones over us be ruling!

O devoted, by doing good works for mankind, bring

rebirth... prepare all this for what's good for all men:

through work in the field, let ox for us be fattening.

The *ruba'i* is a poem of four lines in which usually the first, second and fourth lines rhyme and sometimes with the *radif* (refrain) after the rhyme words… sometimes all four rhyme. It is composed in metres called *ruba'i* metres. Each *ruba'i* is a separate poem in itself and should not be regarded as a part of a long poem as was created by FitzGerald when he translated those he attributed to Omar Khayyam.

The *ruba'i* (as its name implies) is two couplets *(beyts)* in length, or four lines *(misra)*. The *ruba'i* is a different metre from those used in Arabic poetry that preceded it.

How was this metre invented? The accepted story of Rudaki (d. 941) creating this new *metre* of the *hazaj* group which is essential to the *ruba'i* is as follows: one New Year's Festival *(Nowruz)* he happened to be strolling in a garden where some children played with nuts and one threw a walnut along a groove in a stick and it jumped out then rolled back again creating a sound and the children shouted with delight in imitation, 'Ghaltan ghaltan hami ravad ta bun-i gau,' *(Ball, ball, surprising hills to end of a brave try)*. Rudaki immediately recognised in the line's metre a new invention and by the repetition four times of the *rhyme* he had quickly created the *ruba'i...* and is considered the first master of this form and the father of classical Persian Poetry.

Shams-e Qais writing two hundred years later about this moment of poetic history and the effect of this new form on the population said the following... "This new poetic form fascinated all classes, rich and poor, ascetic and drunken rebel-outsider/rend/, all wanted to participate in it... the sinful and the good both loved it; those who were so ignorant they couldn't make out the difference between poetry and prose began to dance to it; those with dead hearts who couldn't tell the difference between a donkey braying and reed's wailing and were a thousand miles away from listening to a lute's strumming, offered up their souls for a *ruba'i*. Many young cloistered girls, from passion for the song of a *ruba'i* broke down the doors and their chastity's walls; many matrons from love for a *ruba'i* let loose the braids of their self-restraint."

And so, the *ruba'i* should be eloquent, spontaneous and ingenious. In the *ruba'i* the first three lines serve as an introduction to the fourth that should be sublime, subtle or pithy and clever. It is also said that the first line is the introduction, the second line and extension of the general theme, the third...

the flight towards the climax, and the fourth a dramatic ending. As can be seen from the quote by Shams-e Qais above, the *ruba'i* immediately appealed to all levels of society and has done so ever since. The nobility and royalty enjoyed those in praise of them and the commoner enjoyed the short, simple homilies... the ascetic and mystic could think upon epigrams of deep religious fervour and wisdom; the reprobates enjoyed the subtle and amusing satires and obscenities... and for everyone, especially the cloistered girls and old maids, many erotic and beautiful love poems to satisfy any passionate heart.

Almost every major and minor poet on the Indo-Pakistan Sub-Continent beginning with Qutub Shah in the 16th century composed at some time in Urdu in the *ruba'i* form, down to the 'undisputed king of the *ruba'i* in the 20th century' Josh Malihabadi.

Note: See 'Comparative Grammar, Lecture 6' in 'Lectures on the Science of Language' 1861 By Max Muller, Reprint Munshi Ram Manohar Lal, Delhi, 1965. The Encyclopaedia Britannica Volume xxi, Eleventh Edition Cambridge 1911 (Pages 246-8).

The *Qit'a* in Persian Poetry

The *qit'a*, which literally means 'fragment', began in Arabic poetry in pre-Islamic times and then passed on to Persian poetry, then Turkish, Urdu and Punjabi and other Eastern poetry. It must consist of at least two couplets and is similar to a *ghazal* or a *qasida* being a monorhyme, with the second lines of the couplets all having the same rhyme... but in the first couplet the double-rhyme does not appear (hence ab, bb, cb, db, eb etc). It can be composed in any metre except that of the *ruba'i*.

It can be a fragment from a *qasida* (a long poem, sometimes hundreds of couplets) or a *ghazal* (usually between seven and fifteen couplets) that are both with the rhyme pattern of aa, ba, ca, da, ea, fa, ga, ha, etc; or... it may be complete in itself, as it most often was.

"The *qit'a* was popular for use in improvisations, a touchstone for new poets, but also a harbour of refuge for their more experienced colleagues, who were so frequently required to dispel the peevishness and boredom of their masters." Jan Rypka (see below).

Sources…

A Literary History of Persia By Edward G. Browne. Volume 2 Cambridge University Press 1902 (Page 34).

Early Persian Poetry by A.V. Williams Jackson: New York. 1920.

Borrowed Ware: Medieval Persian Epigrams, Translated by Dick Davis. Mage Publishers, 1997.(Page 23).

History of Iranian Literature: Jan Rypka et al. D. Reidel Publishing Company Holland 1968. (Pages 95-6).

The *Qasida* in Persian Poetry

This kind of poem resembles a *ghazal* in many ways except that it is longer than the *ghazal* and is often as long as a hundred couplets. In the first couplet, both the lines rhyme, and the same rhyme runs through the whole poem, the rhyme-word being at the end of the second line of each couplet (after the first couplet) as in the *ghazal*. The *qasida* is usually written in praise of someone and is often read in his or her presence, so it is stated that it shouldn't be too long or it might weary the listener. It has a number of sections: i. *matla* - the beginning, ii. *taghazzul* - introduction, iii. *guriz* - the couplets in praise of whoever it is written to, iv. *maqta*- the end. In the *qasida*, the *takhallus* or pen-name of the poet usually does not appear, and if it does it is not necessarily near the end or at the end as in the *ghazal*. Any metre may be used except that used for the *ruba'i* .

The *Masnavi* in Persian Poetry

The *masnavi* is the form used in Persian poetry to write epic ballads or romances. Each couplet has a different rhyme with both lines rhyming. This is to allow the poet greater freedom to go into a longer description of the subject he has chosen to present. All of the great long narrative poems of Persia and Turkey were composed in this form that is a Persian invention and is not known in classical Arabic poetry. The most famous poems written in this form are the 'Shahnama' (Epic of the Kings) of Firdausi, the 'Five Treasures' of Nizami, the 'Seven Thrones' of Jami and the great 6 volume 'Masnavi' of Rumi and the many masnavis of Amir Khusrau.

In the 'Book of the Winebringer' *masnavi,* Hafiz uses a device in relation to the *masnavi* form invented by Nizami in his epic poem *Layla & Majnun.* It is an internal rhyme structure in most of the couplets by beginning many of them with "Winebringer, come" or "Give," and produces a kind of chant that is not dissimilar to the repetition of a word or words that he places at the end of many of his *ghazals.*

Ghazals…

You, desiring to make trouble in crowds and in
privacy,
when You are in crowds You talk but are silent
privately!
Your loving, heart-stealing beauty has as its attributes
waving curls and waist, hair-thin, of this world
manifestly!
Your ones stricken by You go on without water or food:
Your ones with everything come to the table not
hungrily!
My cries don't underestimate, destined in pre-eternity:
they'll revolutionize millstones of seven planes,
heavenly.
Good actions and wisdom are not ours, but we're full
of Your love; drunk, with wine we break fast…
continually.
Be entrusting paradise to Ghalib… for he'd be in that
garden as a nightingale in rapture, singing a new
melody!

It was our silence that the idols was spoiling,

or our crying would never have been happening.

We are obligated as far as we are trustworthy:

by such a way as this others we are perceiving.

Why is this spring causing such an agitation?

Fear of You the heart of autumn was bleeding.

This tumultuous life we cannot fight against:

sighs reins we take, give to hands of grieving!

Seeking paradise's garden in our intoxication,

our idea was realized in dust of Your walking.

O Your door's dust, *Kaaba,* of Ghalib's soul,

from Your Grace is the world worth anything.

Path's thorn clutches like a friend at the clothing

of ours...

all the time it was in there hiding is the thinking

of ours.

I'm like wine in bottle but not of the bottle without You:

soul is not properly mixed in this body, waiting,

of ours.

Oasis gives relief and pleasure in the desert for a time...

if impatience to reach goal is not peace robbing,

of ours.

In a useless attempt to be saving its life an ant will fly...

what lightning will destroy harvest's gathering

of ours?

Our claim for love can anyone doubt when heart's blood

is trying to out of the jugular vein be seeping...

of ours?

Our poetry due to its subtlety cannot be written down:

no dust rises from the steed that goes on racing,

of ours.

Beaks stained with liver's blood parrots sad songs try

to say... they drink liver's blood, songs envying

of ours.

O Ghalib, we did not agree to accept this condition;

poetry was wanting to be the art overwhelming,

of ours.

In exile's dust, the holder of our own mirror

we are..

that is, in our homeland a helpless non-doer

we are.

From music of our bliss don't expect another melody:

sound of snapping of our strings the recorder

we are.

So loved was longing for the rose, that, rose-garden

and the spring and bloodstained altogether,

we are!

In our self we're absorbed, heart with heart involved:

it could be said that attack on our fake affair

we are.

We dissolved in our tears, like a fermented droplet...

but we remain, skirt-front opened, a revealer

we are.

A handful of dust we are, thrown in each direction:

in this world, Lord, what worth, O Reckoner,

we are?

Whatever way you've treated me I thank myself...

even if you complain, thankful to this loser...

we are!

We still desire you even when we should lament:

like moth to lamp on our tomb a night-flyer

we are.

With blood of our liver our life's dust's leavened:

so, to worthless, flying dust adding colour

we are.

To one's own ambition each one is the witness:

a companion to our intoxication and fever

we are.

Like string of pearls is glance's thread behind...

of our own blistered feet the hard walker,

we are.

Ghalib, in thought's mirror like one and image

us we are, yet our Self yet to encounter,

we are.

With a word said with a loving look, me be robbing

you cannot...

with sway of your imagined waist, me be deceiving

you cannot.

About the anguish in my heart there has to be a story...

and by that half a nod of your head, me be tricking

you cannot.

The claim that I am infatuated? No... it is not possible!

Why would I be enraptured when me be fascinating

you cannot?

And although the night of separation has no morning,

all of this talk about the morning me be deceiving,

you cannot.

Only through the tear in the veil do I see the Friend...

even through peephole in the door me be tricking,

you cannot!

O Ghalib, this is my nature... or, I'm not such a one

who believes in hoping for a sign, me be fooling

you cannot!

Go! Be a guide to way of those who went astray,

perceive

when you at times look causing turmoil or affray

perceive.

Seen and behind screen this world's a mirror of secrets:

if mind can't understand this then look its way,

perceive!

If you can't see what things mean, they still are there:

beauty under turban of curls in sweet disarray,

perceive.

I am burnt up by depression... desire, where are you?

In flutter of sigh's wing my breath blown away

perceive.

Our frustrated desire to see you mirrors our state...

show you to yourself and with a look us today

perceive.

Scar of ill luck of frustrated desire is union's mirror:

if a bright night you want, darkness of the day

perceive.

Don't waste free time, think of it as sent by God...

if spring's dawn isn't here, moon's light, I say:

"Perceive!"

Ah no, Ghalib has to go through hopes and fears:

either kill with sword or with a glance slay...

perceive.

Morning is blossoming and rose is awakening,

do no sleep...

now many a flower of perception be gathering,

do not sleep.

With breeze blowing rose's scent, sense of smell ease:

dawn's perfumed air is fresh, gently stirring...

do not sleep!

Before you seek cup of morning know yourself inside:

from your lip last night's wine keeps dripping,

do not sleep!

Vision of Friend morning star gives the good news:

see how the sky's eyes continues its blinking,

do not sleep!

You're deep in sleep and for stars morning grieves:

back of hand from regret its teeth are gnawing,

do not sleep!

Through sighs to hyacinth breath offers a hello...

get up, bloody eyelashes tulips are plucking,

do not sleep!

Delightful to the ear is the gurgling of the bottle:

come here, the bottle to be empty is waiting,

do not sleep!

Being agitated is a sign of life in heart, its beat!

On mirror of the eye, sight is the polishing!

Do not sleep!

Worth of friends in eyes be opened, don't shut!

For friends heart be restless to be helping:

do not sleep!

One wants to keep vigil when death is near...

if of Ghalib a tale you want to be hearing,

do not sleep!

Your beauty put on a veil from sin that shames,

of who...

loving ways are endangered from fiery glances,

of who?

You go into the rose-garden drunk, no veil upon face...

spring's heart became blood-stained from sighs,

of who?

To you we are friendly but you are a stranger to us...

before you and God I ask finally world is witness

of who?

I am becoming envious of the light in others eyes...

knowing well it's from the pathway's dustiness

of who?

You sleep near me provocatively... I'm unaffected

by jealously of rival's thoughts of sensuousness

of who?

At the time of sacrifice I'm shaking with ecstasy:

but, fault not to the sword have sharpened, is

of who?

That you stole my heart with coquetry is obvious…

and not,

in this… you have to know of you I am suspicious,

and not!

My longing becomes so deep, when of my grief I tell you

and from head to foot I talk and still I'm conscious

and not.

In my life your command is law, you are in my actions:

before and behind each veil it is passing… it goes,

and not.

It's said you've enticed even saints and so I am proud:

a kiss is your mouth's message and yet it exists…

and not!

We're sad about the rose-garden as spring's so short:

autumn's furnace makes us happy, yet autumn is,

and not!

Every drop that is lost in the ocean is wealth that's

like something is lost… but, in reality it is a loss

and not!

Humanity is new again with each blink of the eye,

we go on seeing it as the same and yet it still is,

and not!

In spring's winds the rose sways into the branch:

it's hidden like wine in the decanter, it exists

and not.

By gaining power a thug doesn't become nobility,

as a stone on a road that is heavy, worthless

and not.

Rip my side open and see my heart's condition!

For how long do I have to tell you how it is,

and not!

Watch out Ghalib… look to your own feelings:

leave the veil of mind, where it is like this…

and not!

Intoxication reveals a way to be staggering:

fell sorry for feet, the head leaves tottering!

The sigh becomes, richer deeper in effect...

your hard heart's a shop for glass-blowing!

You've stolen my faith, reason and my soul:

what you took is a tale that all are knowing.

Heart's obligation one cannot always take:

thank God our moans no one is answering.

One drops leaves another the rose petals...

passing away are both autumn and spring.

Your 'less' Ghalib takes, and has 'more'...

a drop by giving up, the pearl is becoming.

Joy of spiritually-minded ones comes from a tavern,

Yours...

Babylon's magic is a chapter in a story to discern...

Yours.

Jamshid's cup, Alexander's mirror, why be mentioning?*

What in the past was, is in Your present to learn...

Yours!

Your knowledge makes it possible for us in this world to

walk in idol-temple, put head on threshold, in turn,

Yours.

You put over us the sky to bring about our destruction:

what it steals from us isn't from riches to return,

Yours.

If my thoughts fly to highest heaven it's not my fault:

steed's swiftness isn't depending on whip to learn,

Yours!

You, fascinated by the old masters of poetry's skills,

don't pour scorn on Ghalib who lives in this time,

yours.

*Note: Jamshid the ancient Persian king was said to have had a winecup in which he could see the world. Alexander had a mirror that also did this. Both are symbols for Universal Mind.

We have much to against a veiled you; all complaining

is nothing…

all mouth is heart's wound, but its tongue for telling…

is nothing.

O beauty, if the truth does not upset you I'd tell you this:

all your flirting, small waist and mouth? It, I'm saying,

is nothing.

In way of the One in each breath of dust life is available:

when my life passes by the grief for it I'll be having…

is nothing.

What left heart was recompensed by many more tears:

in love, the difference between winning and losing,

is nothing.

You world seekers, all fighting is baseless, so be upset:

all our freedom or our imprisonment I'm explaining:

is nothing!

This world's a mirror of Being, so where is non-being?

Ocean's as far as eye sees and shore, I'm believing,

is nothing.

Under veil of infamy of Mansur* a sweet voice sings:

from those in seclusion of His secret any revealing

is nothing.

O Ghalib, throw out all unreal ideas imprisoning you:

by God, this world, its good and bad, I'm swearing:

"Is nothing!"

*Note: The Perfect Master and martyr Mansur Hallaj (d.919 A.D.), who was
sentenced to death for saying: "I am the Truth (Anal Haq)." Much has been
written about Hallaj and his famous (and infamous) statement. If the reader
wishes to follow up his life and writings, a list is given below. 'Muslim Saints
and Mystics' by Farid ud-Din Attar trans. by A.J. Arberry R.K.P. pp. 264-272;
'The Kashf al-Mahjub: The Oldest Persian Treatise on Sufism' by Hujwiri.
trans. by R.A. Nicholson, Luzac, U.K. 'Diwan of al Hallaj' trans. into French by
Louis Massignon, Paris 1955 (Documents Spiritual S.10); 'The Passion of Hallaj'
by Louis Massignon, Princeton University Press. For his poems see my 'Mansur
Hallaj: Selected Poems' New Humanity Books, Campbells Creek, 2012.*

Having lost joy's means, heart is anxious for bread:
if the garden is barren it becomes field to be farmed.
It's true from your ignoring me I gain only strength:
your look's cruel coolness by me cannot be matched.
We were known like Majnun from our mad wisdom:
we told our grief's secret in a way it wasn't revealed.
That love is of no comfort is the hardship that I bear:
my soul finds difficult that work easy to be fulfilled.
Why be asking why I am amazed to be seeing you?
My sight's lost in bliss and in eyelashes transfixed.
Turmoil's heat is from us... see how existence boils!
From dust's veil's resurrection, into us transmuted!
I glory in my work's style... it brings me happiness:
the opening of the garment by coat isn't contained.
For God's sake, O idols, circle around the heart; if
Ghalib becomes a Muslim will temple be entered?

They, in darkness of night, happy news of morning

gave me…

They, snuffed out candle and sun's sign, shining…

gave me.

They revealed face and my muttering mouth closed…

They stole heart but eyes that are now expecting,

gave me.

They gave me fiery breath from fire-temple burnt up:

They destroyed idol-temple, its bell's sad ringing,

gave me.

They took the pearls from kings of Iran's banners…

and from them They this pen, pearl-scattering,

gave me.

They, from Afrasayab's Turks took crowns, then

speech of Kayanian kings glory and bearing…

gave me.

What They've plundered of the wealth of Fars…

They in form of tongue that goes on moaning

gave me.

O Ghalib, I'm in fear and danger from the first:

They fate of Sagittarius, Cancer's reckoning

gave me.

When in Love, of the two worlds without a care

one should be…

destroying gross wants and being real, There…

one should be!

Delights spare change spill on aspiration's breast,

sewing worthlessness on soul's crying despair

one should be.

Longing one shouldn't reveal as idle talk from lips:

a veil over secrets of heart, holding with care

one should be.

Preparing to be annihilating even one's own self,

and after to be into flirtation's steamy air…

one should be.

One should feel proud when wings love spreads;

when weakness is glorious, being in despair

one should be.

One should stagger in courtyard of winehouse:

in monastery's corner wrapped up in prayer

one should be.

One shouldn't live drenched in blood of insight:

for those long eyelashes it's only a martyr

one should be.

From that eye that's woken up be seeking light:

a dervish begging at doors open to fresh air

one should be.

Ghalib, you'll have what honour from freedom?

You, for world's finery still want a share!

One, should be?

Fearing your ways, my breath a thread, twisted,

resembles...

that look from your fiery face, hair that is signed

resembles.

Because of heart's foaming in water it is clearly still stuck...

drops of blood on eyelashes rose-buds, scattered,

resembles.

Frustrated desire for your loving makes rose and tulip sway:

bed of roses resurrection of hearts, blood-stained,

resembles.

That one's delirious, ravished by own eyes seen in a mirror:

heat of passion of look, hunter who deer sighted,

resembles.

From path dust rises, reaching height of the crystal heaven:

by fire of madness, the wild my heart tormented

resembles.

Where you do gracefully go, that glorious sight we become:

holding mirror of desire, my eye a heart, sighted,

resembles.

When my grief for you is life-giving, why be sad, worried?

Body, peaceful soul in your street is intoxicated,

resembles.

In court of your glorious sensuality spring's colour, scent,

beggars who gather money to have you guarded

resembles.

See, I'm still faithful! My rival from path has taken you!

Your lane's dust in eyes like eyelashes clogged,

resembles.

World's smoke of madness Ghalib defends himself from:

you could say heaven's vault a head, distracted,

resembles.

When you walk on the earth it becomes the sky:

who sits near your street, is in paradise on high.

Your name is so on my lips, if I kiss a rose-bud

it becomes rare stone of your seal... I do not lie!

If moon thinks it is not that, it becomes less...

moon waxes, so to be your forehead it does try!

Resurrections by hundreds are melted into one

so that they can be the ferment for heart to fry.

My agitated heart's fire I bring and I say this:

"Ah no, what do I have to do to assure you of

this grief due to separation that feeling am I?"

I turn, twist, feed upon grief due to my poems:

I'd steal hearts, if grief for you there, I did spy.

Your wonderful form only aware hearts affect:

if I find others are desiring you, I fall into fire.

Eyes and heart I gave up so my art's admired:

who is there like your knowing, seeing one: I?

What is faith, infidelity, but being's hatred?

Make pure you, so on infidelity you can rely.

Your nature comes from hell's fire O Ghalib:

ah no for that last breath, for after you'll die!

Last night I complained about my sad destiny

to you...

my sight was to the sky, but address of me...

"To you!"

To all that is happening to me, I am like that knot

that is knot knitting your brow, obviously...

'to you!'

Is it a wonder God was lost creating your mouth?

He, was bewildered by your face's beauty...

"To you!"

I burn up paradise with my breath, so rivals don't

know that at end of your lane it says clearly:

'To you!'

I became doubtful by the spring's breeze arrival...

roses and buds your caravan's scent did see:

'To you!'

Before maid-in-waiting taught you bad manners,

on your lap's mirror was seen each illusory:

'To you!'

By grave, after death, tulips and roses blossom...

in Ghalib's heart full was desire to face see!

To... you!

Freedom is a musical instrument with a sound?

No!

Each path we've trod there's an echo profound?

No!

Your weakness and beauty and even drunken pride...

hatred, intolerance, faith, I will not find sound,

no!

One who gives up heart for agony is one so happy...

this field of this world, sowed... is unlimited...

no?

One's self squeeze until wine inside intoxicates...

flagon can't appear in our close group, it's said:

"No!"

Why be sad... at the violence of footsteps of man?

In this world's ways for rose is no cash, dead:

no!

In heart's tumult, a hundred songs, will happen...

but, it is said sick lover to find goal of dread?

No?

From my pen falls every mournful poem of mine:

but of love's song my pen nothing has held.

No?

One giving up life for you death does not fear...

who has body for death has fear to be killed?

No?

I told that one, be merciful to yourself or else...

this heart is so weak, but it can't be stilled!

No?

Your vanity and kindness makes world stop...

God, don't let that one make me oppressed!

No!

That one has dark eyes, never looks our way...

has face fair as moon, but for us, it is said:

"No!"

Rosebud's like your ruby lip but doesn't talk:

narcissus is like your eyes, but is modest?

No!

Earth its water melts, rain a hot atmosphere:

by Ghalib's death I say of Delhi's climate:

"No!"

Come, and my great longing to be at You gazing

see...

my tears off the tips of the eyelashes trickling...

see!

You went from me because I was in such a restless state:

come to my graveside and how I'm now resting

see.

My state's beyond any cure, envy of others shames you?

I'm not among those at Your union's gathering

see!

I've been told You won't look my way, I don't despair...

yes, me I heard You will not see: I am hearing,

see?

Seed did sprout and become a tree and birds nest in it...

but, expecting the Anka* the trap I'm placing,

see?

You don't see how us frustrated lovers beg and pray...

look through my eyes, how at You I'm seeking

see.

If You want to witness the rose-garden in full bloom

come and my condition of in blood drowning,

see!

That hair was split at tips of curls is comb's tyranny:

back of my hand with my teeth I am biting...

see!

My spring You should be and see me blooming fully:

secretly come, how cup of wine I'm draining,

see.

You weren't just to me, I died I was so sick with love:

I want compensation, You were so uncaring!

See?

Ghalib: "I will not without courtesy, be courteous...

how I bend in shadow of Your sword, curving,

see!"

*Note: Anka is the divine bird symbol... God in the Beyond State.

Out of a hundred thousand *houries,* I don't desire

one...

of all the world's beauties only one lights my fire,

one.

In that One's diversity is the clue to that One's unity...

of all numbers beyond counting, unifying figure:

one!

About my heart and soul that are apart of my existence

what to say? One's desperate and in a quagmire,

one.

Lightning of two troublesome disasters They hid in this

handful of dust... one fate and free will's desire,

one.

Ghalib, this land that is called Delhi I can't be leaving:

here, to be of humble ones in the dust I aspire,

one.

With eloquent words in my *Divan* they intoxicated

will be...

because of a lack of wine-drinkers, this wine, aged,

will be.

My star is now accepted in eternity without beginning...

but, in this world after I pass my poetry accepted

will be.

Then, eyes of the blind will hold mirrors of pretension...

the curls of poetry by the paralysed hand combed

will be.

Content's beloved, now the citizen of the heart and soul,

in the country of taste a wanderer, foul-mouthed

will be.

Bitten away by the dark will be the light of life's candle,

and rug of the gathering of drunkards, crumpled

will be.

And a veil will fall over the face of human cooperation:

Christian and Muslim individuality usurped...

will be.

O Ghalib, I built a winehouse in each word's heart...

with eloquent words in my *Divan* they intoxicated

will be!

My heart with soul, in love, from you separated,
       trembles;
like that bird that can see its nest being burned...
       trembles!
When union arrives I'm like thief finding a treasure chest:
       the heart of this one that's so afraid of the guard,
       trembles!
Beloved is so simple-hearted, what can a heart hope for?
       If one should happen to kiss that mouth, beloved
       trembles.
With fluttering lashes you look drunk... glances so hot!
       Accidently arrow my bow shoots, one targeted...
       trembles.
In tasting a soft melody's joy, preacher is not ecstatic;
       but, that one on thinking of a death unexpected,
       trembles.
Ah no, miserly money-changer's regret when in shop
       counterfeit coins are brought... that one's head
       trembles!
If in head of Ghalib is no madness, why give up life?
       Why when prostrating on threshold, forehead
       trembles?

You enjoy creating tumult, privately and openly:

You speak in the crowd, alone You act inwardly.

In taking hearts Your loving beauty has helpers:

long, wavy curls, hair-thin waist of world to see!

Your poor ones caravan has no food, no water...

as Your rich ones at table are never ever hungry.

My tears don't underestimate, my fate it is so...

such a stream makes turn millstones of eternity!

We've no deeds or wisdom, yet full of Your love:

we're always drunk, fast with wine breaks easy.

To Ghalib grant paradise, in its garden this one

would be a nightingale in rapture, a new melody!

This silence of ours causes idols to be spoiled...
in the past our lamenting some results ensured!
We're obliged to be constant to have any effect:
the worthiness of others this way has revealed.
Why has nature of the spring agitated become?
It's like fearing You autumn's heart's bloodied!
Life's tumult we have no more strength to fight:
from sighs we took reins, to grief them handed.
We sought paradise's rose-garden by drinking:
Your graceful walk sobered us, by dust raised!
Your door's dust is *Kaaba* of Ghalib's heart...
due to Your grace beauty in this world existed.

As spacious as our breast's field, rose-garden…

is not:

if from Your sword not wounded, a heart open

is not!

I'm burning, but I'm afraid that the fire might lessen:

it's a shame on fire water of life having effect on

is not.

I have been near death for so long, but still I can't die:

in Your tyranny's realm decree of death written

is not.

For our heart's misery even paradise has no remedy:

the way it's set-up any help to our state given…

is not.

Friend's kindness or wrath, either we're accepting:

this thought is a mirror's image, it to happen…

is not.

Don't beg relief from salve even if Ghalib's body

is wounded all over by Friend: beggar this one

is not!

In that valley where even walking stick of Khizer

is asleep,*

I go on travelling on breast as each foot's slipper

is asleep.

I've come to Your home of loving with this entreaty...

but, in shade of royal palace's wall this beggar

is asleep!

Last Day's dawn rising mean, black-faced from grave

is complainer of heart-ache, pill-seeker, after...

is asleep!

Wind changes, pitch-black night, sea by storm lashed:

broken is that anchor, and this ship's master...

is asleep!

Heart trembles at beads, prayer-mat, patched coat...

awake is road's robber, as pious and the lover...

is asleep!

Not all the tale are night's length, me being awake:

one should bring news of my fate, or it, brother,

is asleep!

From a distance look, don't try to be near the king:*

see that the window is open but dragon at door

is asleep!

All seeing the way that I am sleeping, is knowing

that in the line of all the caravans the leader...

is asleep.

From safety of path what joy is from *Kaaba* being

near if camel can't walk, each of my feet I fear,

is asleep?

*Notes: Khizer is often called: "The Green One" for he was said to have drunk from the Fountain of Immortality and gained Eternal life. He has been identified with Elias, St. George, Phineas, the Angel Gabriel, the companion of Mohammed on a journey which is told in the Koran, viii, 59-81, and throughout the literature of Mysticism has appeared to many great seekers who eventually became Masters. See my 'Khidr in Sufi Poetry' New Humanity Books, 2012.
*The king referred to here is most likely Bahadur Shah Zafar (1775-1862) the last of the Mughal emperors in India, as well as the last ruler of the Timurid Dynasty. He presided over a Mughal empire that barely extended beyond Delhi's Red Fort. The British Raj was the dominant political and military power in 19th-century India. When the victory of the British became certain, Zafar took refuge at Humayun's Tomb, in an area that was then at the outskirts of Delhi, and hid there. British forces led by Major Hodson surrounded the tomb and compelled his surrender. He was exiled to Rangoon. Modern India views him as one of its first nationalists, someone who actively opposed British rule in India. In 1959, the All India Bahadur Shah Zafar Academy was founded expressly to spread awareness about his contribution to the first national freedom movement of India. Several movies in Hindi/Urdu have depicted his role during the rebellion of 1857. There are roads bearing his name in New Delhi and other cities. Zafar was a noted Urdu poet and Sufi who often held poetry readings at his court that the poets Zauq, Ghalib, Momin, Shefta and Dagh often attended. He was especially influenced by the poet Zauq. He wrote a large number of Urdu ghazals, ruba'is, qit'as and other forms of poetry. After the demise of Zauq, it was Ghalib who became his mentor. See my: Bahadur Shah Zafar, Sufi Poet & Last Mughal Emperor & His Circle of Poets...Zauq, Ghalib, Momin, Shefta, Dagh, Selected Poems, New Humanity Books, 2017.

I'm a lover, no question of disgrace or reputation:
usual practice in such cases is... no confrontation!
That one who drinks wine with Friend in private,
knows about *houri,* Kausar, Paradise's location. *
Wine's the one cure for our heart that's afflicted:
why talk 'lawful, unlawful' to who cannot go on?
I've no fear of my dark night in these dark days...
when no dawn, do I know when us dusk's upon?
You said: 'Cage is fine, you can open feathers'...
say, for all tired of its noose, where is salvation?
Rising dust from galloping steed is a good sign:
messenger, tell what Love's fine lips passed on!
Benvolent's bowl gives me only the fate of dust:
the sky's destiny from this bowl is what portion?
You award virtue, for good deeds we ask no pay:
if bad nature is from You too, why... retribution?
If cloak and the *Koran* Ghalib has not yet sold...
why in market ask, 'How much is rare red wine?'

*Notes A houri is a beautiful maiden of Paradise.
Kausar is a river in Paradise.*

Your bright beauty sight's riches plunders insolently:
Your slow stroll tramples lovers' heads, impudently!
Your desire's scar, is busy in decorating the hearts...
sword's wound roams river's play-ground, brazenly!
Careful... agony that is caused by Your cruelty has
made sighs that lament becomes even more cheeky!
Those others desire for union do not serious take...
asking at doors here is a beggar who acts blatantly.
That rival could not see you privately, I enjoyed...
then I saw that one speak to you in street, openly!
I feel sorry for a hand struggling to open the front:
with your pure skirt it has been brazen, obviously!
From your curls what help can a worried heart get?
They're so saucy they encircle your waist cheekily!
Before Ghalib the parrots are scattering sweetness
as lips words are impudent in taking sugar sweetly.

I've to say this, though that one how to listen,

doesn't know...

to my night is a morning but it how to dawn,

doesn't know.

From chains how can I free self and escape the cage?

We're like that deer that how to be soon gone

doesn't know.

From that one's message we regain pleasure of sight:

our desire sight or sound, difference between

doesn't know.

You come out on display with all of that flirtation...

don't think we've mirror's eyes that to see in

doesn't know.

To take that red wine from the flagon is my desire...

it, to ask for the cup from winbringer to bring

doesn't know.

Ghalib made self in way of grief that delights you:

heart's made but one its restlessness define,

doesn't know.

All who are longing for union with the Beloved...
to be one with that One self must be annihilated!
One mad without thread removes one from front
of coat so as to a rend in garment make mended.
On neck is blood of a thousand innocent victims
of any who say that the beauties are doing good!
Mirage is water to whose lips crack with thirst:
if all seems real it's an exaggeration understood.
From the desire to see Your face spring's drunk:
Your scent arrives if we smell mouth of rosebud!
Ghalib can't be marked with stain of hypocrisy:
clean is the patched coat that in wine is washed!

Musical instrument is freedom, but sound it's making

is none...

whatever road we took, of echo our steps were taking,

is none!

Beauty, drunken arrogance, love, weakness... all happened:

cruelty I can't take; in you faith, tolerance happening

is none!

That one's truly happy who to pain is abandoning heart...

meadow is world's field that's sown, fence enclosing

is none!

Until you're drunk on wine within, your being squeeze...

for goblet in our party that's closed, need for having

is none.

O grass by the path, why cry over footsteps of mankind?

Even for rose, in use of world, blood-money offering

is none!

A hundred tunes are born within the heart inner tumult:

but we could say to reach goal sigh lover is sighing

is none!

From my pen falling all first couplets of poem are cries:

but love's melody my musical instrument's playing

is none!

Who sheds life grieving for You, death will not catch…

fear of that for one who to calamity body is tossing

is none!

I told that one to be merciful to self, or do what is best:

I've heart that strength left to oppression be taking

is none!

Due to that one's conceit, kindness is worldly cruelty:

O Lord, make sure that one's cruelty to me coming

is none!

That one has black eyes and is never looking this way:

that one's a bright moon-like face, but our viewing

is none!

Your ruby lips are like the rosebud, but it doesn't talk:

eyes are like narcissus but its modesty, blushing…

is none!

Earth is melted by its water, a hot vapour is its rain:

by Ghalib's death, Delhi's climate good having,

is none!

The revolution of the times our sadness affecting

is not:

in this day that is dark any morning or evening…

is not!

The lips of the heart-stealer I kiss, but don't dare to bite:

heart's soft, so courage to this desire be fulfilling,

is not.

Because of that one, in air each mote of my dust dances:

of madness of love, it is true that a time ending

is not!

Into calamity throw yourself, so calamity you don't fear:

the fear of the trap the bird in cage still suffering

is not.

See nightingale in the rosegarden and moth in the crowd:

even in union love any bit of satisfaction finding,

is not!

To the need of the drinker every drop of wine is poured…

barrels of flagons in winehouse of grace, flowing

is not!

From Friend separated we threw dust upon our head,

even though on that road a hundred streams flowed.

By stopped desire to see You, my tears tears well up:

around pearl, my glance is that lustre, that is wound!

Friend can give whatever of hell or paradise, already

I have delight thinking of them and my liver's scared.

It cannot be contained in the garden it has grown so,

cypress that from desire for You, to chest is pressed!

A whole life longing for You was a treasure of grief:

see now how we've to You for You to enjoy, handed!

Ghazal is being sung by the minstrel, Ghalib hears:

winebringer, from circle of friends take wine, I said.

Know my devotion to You, seek proof from others...

be aware of cruelties You heaped on heart and head.

What did my soul see in Your eyes filled with wine:

what devastation in my head has Your hair worked?

In Your world You have a thousand afflicted ones...

just show a little care to Ghalib, worn out, languid!

O heart, from that rosebush of hope any sign

bring me…

an autumn leaf if fresh rose isn't to be mine,

bring me!

O deep love, heart hasn't opened from fear of grief:

calamity from source of tumult's mad design

bring me.

O destiny, that I am not the target I'm admitting:

occasionally, arrow shot by Your bow so fine

bring me.

You who to lover no letter from that one did bring:

the news of union from that mouth this time

bring me!

Grieving for You all have given up life, jealously…

don't kill by jealousy, by grief of all as mine,

bring me!

O God, You brought this existence from nothing:

kisses from treasure of that mouth in illusion

bring me.

Ghalib, my heart is not deceived by simple words:

the unusual ways of intricate versification

bring me!

Upon my heart the breath of affliction

bring...

me, out of my self, like a lamentation,

bring!

Make this desire's worth even more, or from

within the depth my longing going on

bring.

Even more bitter than death, my life's been:

death now more likeable than this one

bring!

Be adorning the colour of the rose garden...

from Azar's blazing flames Abraham

bring!*

From gratitude the lips keep giving pearls:

hearts rich from grief's accumulation,

bring.

Ghalib is agreeing with Naziri who said...

'Rob what drops and pearl's location

bring.'*

*Note: Abraham was thrown into the fire on God's orders by his father idol-maker Azar, but was saved by God. *Naziri (d. 1614) is said to have advanced the ghazal and his Divan still is popular throughout the sub-continent. His reputation as a ghazal writer was so great that Sa'ib thought he was greater than himself and 'Urfi and his style was later imitated by Ghalib.
See my 'Poetry of India, New Humanity Books 2013... pages 361-368 .

That very delicate one, face in the dust is resting,

see...

lying on wet dirt, restlessly the breast is beating,

see!

Lightning that burnt men's souls now makes heart cold:

that flirt once drew blood, palms henna fading...

see!

That one who even in private didn't ask God to forgive;

now due to the sky's tyranny, all that lamenting

see!

If one talks of grief, that one... "A river's between us!"

a bloody river from those eyes, others shedding,

see!

Breast that like soul stayed hidden from world's eyes:

shown at a window with dress front's opening,

see!

Ears follow prey's sound when still chasing the game:

eyes on game-straps when back steed turning,

see!

See gratitude to doorkeeper on another's threshold...

that envy of rubbish in a street 'unbecoming',

see!

Hear that one reproaching self, see the smile on lips:

antidote for the poison that one is swallowing

see!

See beauty of those eyes and the perfection of heart:

nature's ardour, eyes pearls shedding, sighing,

see!

Mornings that one says Ghalib's poems hopefully:

that one allow, such excellence, understanding,

see!

A dark curtain vapour's smoke made and firmament

I called it...

at horrible dream eyes clashed and world in ferment

I called it!

In eyes fantasy threw dust, wilderness of discontent

I called it...

drop melted and ocean without shore to circumvent

I called it!

Against fire wind brushed skirt and spring's advent

I called it:

by intoxication flame became scar, autumn's event

I called it!

In foreign land feeling alone, to my country I went,

I called it:

when too narrow was snare's noose nest of torment

I called it!

Made with dignity in my chest my heart of content

I called it:

it disappeared to such a flirt that life, inconvenient,

I called it!

One was so quick to kill me that murderous intent

I called it:

that I ever called that one cruel, it was not meant,

I called it!

So that by my grateful slavery I could please that one,

though master of my house, that guest's consent,

I called it.

Secret friendship heart did not want tongue to know...

I said 'so and so' or 'such and such' as a non-event

I called it!

Indifference is a killer and soul by a glance is stolen...

one is the sword's lustre, or back of bow, so bent,

I called it.

Whatever happens in this spiritual path, will pass...

the *Kaaba* I saw, the travellers' footprint, spent,

I called it.

To follow path of patience, I've lived on that hope...

from me You've cut You, but as trial of torment

I called it!

In the garden of Ajam,*Ghalib was a nightingale...

in my ignorance as India's parrot of the orient

I named it!

*Note: Ajam means 'Persia'.

96

Happy at disaster, like bridge in torrent's reflection:

dance!

Separating Self from self, yourself balance... go on,

dance!

No faith keeping promises, what joy comes is fortunate!

When making promises if beauties offer adulation:

dance!

Why talk of ending journey, all delight is in the search!

Lose balance when camel's bell tells of the location:

dance!

When with pride we walked into garden it was green...

O fire, in burning of our rubbish and straw keep on,

dance!

Listen to the owl's hooting as some kind of song too...

to breeze from fluttering of phoenix's wings listen,

dance!

In love can't be found delight of a desert's wasteland:

a twister of dust become and rising in air... spin!

Dance!

Of respected friends put away their out-dated ways...

at wedding feast mourn, in crowd that mourn...

dance!

Unlike friendship of hypocrites or anger of the pious,

do not be full of self, before each and everyone

dance!

Don't look for joy in blooming or distress in burning,

on edge of hot wind, soft breeze, in exaltation

dance!

Ghalib, to whom are you tied with in of all this joy?

In chains of calamity be more in Self, as one...

dance!

To on that promise of your tongue be relying

was wrong, so wrong:

we could see that the way you were talking

was wrong, so wrong!

I've gazed closely at the bud, it has its own grace...

but to say that your mouth it's resembling

was wrong, so wrong.

A great mistake to believe you'd send a message...

from your lips to seek to desire be fulfilling

was wrong, so wrong!

Reward for my trust, even now it's your tyranny:

of you being suspicious, our complaining

was wrong, so wrong!

O bright creation of many colours where are you?

In world what sign of you was showing

was wrong, so wrong!

The threads of illusion deep love wished to twist:

or an idea of your waist and our existing

was wrong, so wrong.

You are that which resembling the nothingness!

shadow thrown by your cypress moving,

was wrong, so wrong.

You want Ghalib to die with this verse on lips?

'Rely on promise your tongue was making

was wrong, so wrong!'

While the lips of that beloved I am kissing

I feel sorry...

while for the fountain of life I'm thirsting

I feel sorry.

In the city of love I am that country bumpkin...

who when in tangled hair coiling, twisting

I feel sorry.

In the anguish of this life to full flavour taste,

I upon heart disasters shed, then for living

I feel sorry!

I am always anxious as I've never left my self:

for Parsis, Muslims, in truth's way going

I feel sorry.

As heart's yours, to body hugs, kisses offer...

for your hidden mercy I should be saying

'I feel sorry?'

Ghalib, I heard it from Naziri who said this:

'For the sky I cry if not for any sighing...

I feel sorry!'*

*Note: Naziri (d. 1614) is said to have advanced the ghazal and his Divan still is popular throughout the sub-continent. His reputation as a ghazal writer was so great that Sa'ib thought he was greater than himself and 'Urfi and his style was later imitated by Ghalib. See my 'Poetry of India, New Humanity Books 2013... pages 361-368.

In strife or when alone, stirred up in change are you,

when no one else is there, you try to talk to... You!

You manifest Your beauty in the ways of love with

complex attributes; like a hair-thin waist, it's true!

Your radiance whets the vision of the visionaries...

it's as that of lightening: like *kohl* in their eyes, too.

In gaining the elixir useless is power of Alexander:

if one doesn't like Khizer, immortality is not new!*

In Your court 'Ali's bleeding wounds are like roses:

bass and treble of Your music is Kerbala, for You!*

Those ill-fated make up caravan of starving seekers:

without wanting food gourmets get sweets... anew!

All these pulses that are aflame with heat Your love

set fire to dry straw that in the clay shows through!

*Note: Hazrat 'Ali was of course the son-in-law of Prophet Mohammed who
was martyred at Kerbala. For Khizer & Alexander see previous notes.

Longing for You I'm addicted to the poison of cruelty:

even in the mouth of the dragon, I enjoy some greenery.

My tears shed in knowledge of eternity do not ignore;

as in their flows movement of seven skies one can see.

I'm full of Your love but without knowledge and piety;

my drunkenness goes on, as breakfast is wine, for me!

To Ghalib give Your Paradise as I'll be in the garden

forever a nightingale, new melodies singing eternally!

In the dust of my exile my own mirror-holder

I am...

or, in my native land seemingly lost forever,

I am!

From the music of my ecstasy be expecting no sound,

as sound of breaking of my own string, here

I am.

In trouble to fulfil my desire for the much-loved rose;

blooming garden for me is blood, of it a giver

I am.

In every direction a handful of dust has been thrown:

Lord, how will be known meaning of whoever

I am?

I'm expected to cry, but... full of the winds of desire,

the moth of the lamp at my tomb is the lover

I am.

With blood of my liver my being's earth is mixed...

beauty of the garment made by me, as wearer

I am.

On this earth each one is aware of one's intentions:

in my ecstasy and my frenzy wrapt as a loner

I am.

Thread of pearls is the thread of the watchful eyes:

of my own blistered feet the faster runner,

I am!

I'm Ghalib, reflecting self in the mirror of thought:

merging and in conflict with self, together

I am!

If you have not any faith in my waiting,

come…

you who argue, no excuses be seeking…

come!

This heart isn't filled by one or two cruelties…

with all available me be annihilating,

come!

By decent ways don't think of killing the crazy:

give up authority, as a wind of spring

come!

You cut off relations with us to be with others:

promise of faithfulness is now nothing,

come!

There is different joy in union and separation…

be off a thousand times, million coming

come!

I'm proud of being in love, it's all that I need…

once to soul hopefully pining, enquiring,

come.

Your nature isn't as delicate as my patience…

my hands and heart are tired of waiting:

come!

Monastery rituals are popular, don't do them:

wealth of the winehouse is in forgetting;

come!

Ghalib, if you are desiring a fortress of safety,

to group of poor drunkards we are being,

come!

In work of waiting for moon in loneliness of night

thread of the rosary of the stars became eyesight!

One can't imagine to on a petal place a dewdrop:

spring also bites lips in useless desire for respite!

I threw myself into depth of the dragon's throat:

from noise of warring aims my soul was uptight!

My ruin fate brought if ever I think of rebuilding,

bricks would like dry bones with no flesh in sight.

Quiet heart I salute you, of desire's ability I brag:

from raging ocean this drop couldn't raise a fight!

I hail giving up, ecstasy, drinking the prohibited:

a dry lip kill what, in mirage of religious might?

One seeing my perspiration thinks I am dead...

one does not know inner fire is sweat of delight!

Ghalib take care, such is like breaking rosary's

thread with God's name, by breath of insight!

Each atom is rapt in that one beauty reflecting,
wondrous six dimensions mirror a bewildering!
I helplessly go along with delaying the ensnarer...
I advise myself, my abode in that snare is lying!
Wander in your imagination, if you don't leave
each world you enter, is another to be entering!
Chains of my self-control are broken by spring:
the rose is the whip to the steed of my desiring!
A destination is each bit in the journey of love:
a shore is every drop in ocean of one's thinking!
How long have I to bear the lies of Your world?
Stuck in world's mire far from You I'm staying!
When to the lovers desire becomes all there is,
way, wind's dust, Love's curl, comb, are being!
Don't worry, a range of pleasures break gloom:
that moon's a lid that a jug of wine is capping!
Ghalib could say in the prison wall is a crevice:
it is eye of abode of gloom, the flood awaiting!

You carried off my heart, yet called the heart-dweller,

You can't...

we may see Your cruelties but be called the tormenter

You can't!

In Your battlefield we don't need to have a spear or sword:

in Your banquet, need to ask for wine, winebringer...

you can't.

That brightness of Your arms and neck one may not see...

to define those adornments of Your bangle and collar

you can't.

One can't call You winebringer when You offer us wine:

new idols You go on offering us yet to call You Azar

you can't. *

From bravery don't expect succour, lightning is sudden:

here, be like a moth and wish to be a salamander...

you can't!

What's the point in moaning when the conflict is over?

Self-hurt ends, on resurrection to be a complainer,

you can't!

I do not seek shade or spring in heat of this going on...

so to be talking to me of Paradise's *tuba* or *kausar*

you can't!

In your breast that secret lying cannot be like a sermon,

on a gibbet it can only be told, in a pulpit as teller,

you can't.*

This man in love of ours is facing a strange dilemma…

Ghalib, who is not a Momin, to call a non-believer

you can't.*

Come, for that order of the sky be changing,

we will...

altering destiny by the heavy cup circulating

we will!

We'll be doting on the spectacle with eye and heart...

with heart, soul, it to our advantage turning

we will.

We'll stay in a corner of winehouse, keep door open:

the policeman on rounds to an alley sending

we will!

We'll not care if there are soldiers to be arrested...

if from king they bring a gift, back it sending

we will!

We'll not talk, if a talker with gods' talks our talk:

if as guest a friend of God comes, off sending

we will.

We'll be stifling the dawn with our being's heat...

from the scorch of the day the world saving,

we will!

If to ravish the garden's trees wood-cutters arrive,

from gate with empty baskets them pushing

we will.

Peacefully… be making the morning's songbirds

go back from grove and to nests be retiring,

we will.

I, Ghalib, can't imagine union with my Beloved:

come, then the destiny of the sky changing

we will!

The dust blowing towards my tomb is stirring

in those veins of my dread is now a beginning.

I'll not raise head from earth until clarion call:

at eyes half-asleep these eyes are still looking.

The messenger's cold sighs are telling silently

the reply... my message no effect was having.

I gave soul wrongly, quickly, and didn't know

that Friend wasn't so fast but quick in taking.

With your gifts keep favouring all of my foes:

me if you can a blister on my breast be giving.

You continue to ask after my health and in it

is a hint that I may put up with more chiding.

You first drink the wine, then be winebringer:

if there is any veil, then your self, it is being!

We're not depressed by the cold of the times:

because of our ruin face of the sun is shining.

Rainy season is India's real spring, O Ghalib:

in our abode of autumn is the time of drinking.

Prohibiting wine for me except for an inquisition

is nothing!

Inquisitor, from grapes but water the extraction

is nothing!

We are adoring beauty, ignoring the pain and pleasure…

even Hell, but a admirable way of suffercation,

is nothing!

Life is really just laziness, when strife stays far away…

the life of Khizer is just more years in addition:

is nothing!

All are the Lord of the grape, a drop, tide, vortex, foam:

this being 'I' and 'we' a concealment, put on…

is nothing!

All who adored the form in vain were finally defamed…

what they say is obvious is really only a curtain,

is nothing!

Life is made beautiful by all this concern that we have:

warp, woof of existence is our writhing in pain,

is nothing!

Wound of my heart's a thirsty lip for Your smile's salt:

each two eyes, two salt-cellars but imagination,

is nothing!

Yourself reveal not as a favour as I'm not even a mote:

but for the shining of atoms the beauty of the sun

is nothing.

Here, a few colourful subtleties and no formalities…

the *Divan* of Ghalib I saw, it is only a selection,

is nothing!

My desire for melody back to me ecstasy bringing

is...

in house of my mind noise of each night fighting

is.

I'll pour it out through my eyes if it doesn't get out itself:

it melts the heart into blood and in breast flaring

is!

You're knowing ways of the wilderness, O shy Friend...

hand me a torch that the wind never extinguising

is!

If Winehouse Master pours from gourd, take it, leave...

if in a flask offered, put on shoulder, joy beginning

is!

In flask sweet basil blooms, with the drips music flows:

lay one to be seen, the other for ears to be hearing

is.

With wine, now with art, make me unconscious of self;

now in dark wine, with song consciousness rising

is!

God, with some new kind of pain acquaint me deeply,

now in walls of my clay many a freedom growing

is.

Each lightning bolt that is able to melt my spectacles

send off and pour it in cup that desire for seeing

is.

Of pain's pleasure the poor man has no knowledge of:

turn me into thorns, in redeemer's the strewing

is!

Under that fearful glance the joy be knowing,

see...

how the frown the glorious forhead is covering

see!

Our actions to you we assigned to us to supervise...

all the talk of love and hate we find insulting,

see!

I grieve that in your waiting fear does not increase:

ambushed, no chase, no trap is to be seeing...

see?

World of ours is beautified by tyranny; each drop

of blood shed on its face is rouge, enhancing,

see!

In love's path the ways of wisdom aren't needed:

traveller's use of feet pity, brow be looking...

see?

One is taking revenge in separation, by removal

of hot blood from heart, my fiery breathing,

see!

Without a veil don't seek the heat of derivation;

my bleeding heart through lashes flowing,

see!

But these changing colours from eternity there's

no creation so garden as mirage blooming

see.

A fire-stone's nature can't be fine without pain:

careful to worth of melancholy's working,

see.

With plectrum striking string of soul harder

I will...

who knows what descant be making louder,

I will?

Within me old passions are once more fighting...

again like one mad, a howl raising crazier,

I will!

Although this heart of mine to no one is bonded

for this or that heart's blood making hotter

I will.

Each desire in my heart I tie it up or I rip it out,

of all images with captions being destroyer

I will.

Even though I talk about all gains of business...

songs of orchards and gardens being singer

I will!

In the tent of old Azar I am keeping my chisel...

in turban of Numan being of tulip the fixer

I will.*

In worship of idols I am asserting my existence:

if I brag about my faith being an unbeliever

I will.

It's said in highway are the hazards of pirates…

so, going on those paths that go nowhere

I will.

Of the ways of the world I know those secrets…

so, laughing at the wise and fools louder…

I will!

*Notes: Azar was the father of Abraham, an idol-maker (see previos notes)
Numan was a philosopher & companion of Prophet Mohammed.

I'm getting up, to the wornout from the beautiful

annihilate…

in meeting of colours and odours a new order I'll

create!

In their ecstasy the sages have no desire for a vision…

I'll bring Venus down with power of my song I

state!

Beloved will shrivel from my nererending sad songs…

rings and ornaments will slip off form at a fast

rate!

Into the heart of madness I will add much disturbance:

with brain of reason I mingle fantasy's winds,

elaborate!

I'm that tree that doesn't bear fruit but for songbirds…

I am that cloud that drops no rain but pearls

immaculate!

Past's heroes will hear tale of my war with inner self:

they'll lose valour as sword loses shine; it'll

eventuate!

In the *Kaaba* my weakness won me a special spot…

I lay mattress as others lay prayer-mats: it's

delicate!

So as to make the vintage more caustic and acrid...

with it I crush glass of flask, and in cup, it I

celebrate!

I, Ghalib, in the rare strain of a lover's high praises

get up to the the wornout from the beautiful

annihilate.

When You gave us riches and with a riot our souls

filled

with Your hands, You... 'What did you do to me?'

enquired.

When unanxious to see expressed Your beauty's strength,

to the eyes of all who see Your Self You still stay

devoted.

In the nature of repentance, there lies seven great fires...

to the criminal it's the real punishment that out is

meted!

To whom You reveal Your face a hundred roads open...

one You keep in hope of tomorrow to real bliss is

led!

By Your inquest in torment further are tormented ones:

by Your kindness, the well-off are nearly always

favoured.

Knowlege of a hundred deserts, You let a grain gain...

knowledge of seven rivers You to a mere droplet

allowed!

From the eyes longing to see You a Tigris bursts forth:

wherever You stay a fire bursts out in that breast

unstopped!

Aspects of the same jewel are form and immanence...

in forms of others Your own spectacle You have

enjoyed!

These eyes weep, this tongue sighs, this heart shouts:

in this one, Ghalib, all of Your secrets You have

revealed.

Heart lost all patience due to your gentle ways…
you keep majestic height dressed in light, always.
You're an inferno due to your unpleasant actions;
but, due to your beautiful face, a paradise stays!
By faith a Zoroastrian, you're a fire-worshipper
a cane-carrier singing sacred songs; it, me flays!
You are so full of gall like a sudden death can be:
you are of little hope like sweet life; never stays!
You are less than rich when you favour another,
in stealing of hearts a begger that never strays!
You are like a burning desert in your vengeance:
you're like a palace-garden in your kindly ways.
You wear a fragrant veil because of your curls…
you've shine of gold by body's radiance always.
You talk about Layla when you speak of you…
tormenting Ghalib you praise Majnun's ways!

My heart in my breast is on fire from weeping,

as if a piece of meat to make *kebab* is roasting!

Dust of caravan is merely sight of many roses,

rising of sun in the east is a drunk's beginning.

With roar of Judgement Day my cry's in tune:

with tumult of a tempest my poems are riding.

From my dust my heart's cry and flame rises...

this way my dust is alive and vision's needing!

Seeing my joy my love's impatient yet humble:

to pride of a killer, answer is sadness of dying!

On morn of union's night heart still hovers...

doors, windows, of your attire keep dreaming.

Of the seven fires my heart and soul are like:

I'd opted for all the six gardens, be listening!

Winebringer, throat thirsty, heart, soul dead:

a cup of wine that has fire in water be giving!

Ghalib, take life, in a soaking spring seek joy:

your garden's beauty's in your youth: nothing!

A visionary is one who gives heart so it's captivated,

dancers of Azar's idols in heart of stone are captured.

So that between wrath and mercy there is no excuse,

You never accepted my thanks or complaints heard!

You, every grain has its face turned towards You...

so, in quest of You, by the desert one can be guided.

All who bear Your wound travel away from heart...

so, You give to another touchstone for to be judged!

As in love's art is no bravery left for rivals to show,

I'm happy there is only You where ever You faced.

Why envy angels, who do not to You find a way?

In Your air they flutter around uselessly, not led!

Ah no, I burn in my blood as it is said You count

each teardrop of my eye and hear all sighs sighed.

If water of *Kausar* is given me it will be just dust:

if *Tuba's* mine I'll use it for fuel, its fruit is used. *

Ritual of warriors in battle is to croon Your name:

my thoughts like Alexander's mirror... is rusted. *

---

*Note: Kausar or Kauther is a river or stream in Paradise and the Tuba is a tree
there.
*Alexander is said to have had a mirror in which he could see antwhere in the
world... a symbol for the sixth plane or Universal Mind.

Ruba'is...

We imagined us a droplet so we lost in us then

became…

from this delusion we were freed, we the ocean

became.

In this world we hide, but we really are its essence…

we lost like the droplet in the surge of the ocean

became.

Proscribing not drinking wine no matter what

have they...

but really telling a lie they think we've forgot,

have they.

Ghalib, you're a Muslim in a fire-temple, said

have they,

but really telling a lie they think you've forgot

have they.

We're at your lane where all life to be living

is;

where we your feet trod... dust to be kissing

is!

To be begging for happiness is to be light in the head:

joyful the heart that great through suffering

is.

Your loving looks magic's spell will be cancelling

like from caravan a robber gets off with nothing!

Your face's colour the spring is wishing to own:

each moment it arghavan's leaves is changing. *

*Note: The leaves of the arghavan or Judas-tree are pink.

If I wear piety's coat, you will not me not see:

with idols up sleeves I am an infidel, secretly.

If my soul and life I never called you... excuse

me, I'm so sure that loving you I'll always be!

Why ask when drunk from your lips what I'm

wanting?

When you are drunk to kiss you, your lips be

sucking!

Who would be consoled if your veil was lifted away?

On your face my look would as your veil be

covering!

Let me be one of the beggars at Your wayside,

the journey is to far and these feet are so tired.

Spark's heat would light up my straw-like face,

so to rose-garden's brightener I'm not obliged.

I'm drunk on madness, now it's spring,

you can kill me…

I've bottle in hand, rose on lap laying,

you can kill me!

I'm kept alive by your indifference, or in your

gathering for uncontrollably crying…

you can kill me.

You tie knots non-stop when so hard I'm

trying,

calamities make swim if my affairs are

flowing.

No jewel I've turned up though in my heart I dug,

I was told the work now the wages be

setting.

O joy, grief, from fear of death you freed me,

to serve life became every suffered difficulty!

"What is death after life?" I asked Wisdom.

It said, "After being awake, a sleep, heavy."

I'm happy preacher and Brahmin on my denial

agree…

with fight between faith and lack of it heart's

easy.

Ghalib why sleep, of self why so unconscious

be?

Pious are at mosque, in rose-garden the drunks,

obviously.

Each blow I can bear, yet my nature is O so

delicate...

I'm a rock; when worked on, as fine glass I

rate!

My loyalty's depressing, Your cruelty embarrassing:

to torture me You try but, O no, not enough

hate!

Without You, as the wine is from the glass

parted…

this soul is in my form but it's not of it, it's

separated!

Ghalib, not through you this state you attained:

poetry came by itself, asked if you as work

accepted!

You're drunk soon, your secret I only too well

know...

drink only one glass and then into my care it

throw!

Come; night of separation is far beyond endurance;

thousand years of life I'd give to not see you

go!

You're totality of all neverending graces of

spring…

your perfume arrives, from each rose I am

smelling!

Enough Ghalib, to friends don't still be a burden:

let the poem you compose, for yourself be

creating!

Dark is the night, far is the goal, path I can't

see...

from joy I die each time I see wine's flashes,

suddenly!

A pride lives locked inside home of my deep

humility...

one can't take drop from its strength to raise

sea!

You have lost colour in love and autumn is it
revealing...
so that all the colours of world's spring is not
matching!
Orator, I'd not die for you, but if you say that name
it'll make a spell that all your words are never
casting!

Never these words came from my lips but they're

true...

you said: 'Beautiful women's hearts stony are...'

true!

My love ask and my desire ask: it's no sin you did say:

in love desire should have no place whatsoever...

true!

I'm pleased by my aching heart, in my patience it

planted

a hopelessness bringing peace that will never be

dead.

All kinds of regrets come by my days that pass by:

in hope's cup they're the dregs of wine that have

settled!

All grief and all pleasure that arrives, are joined

together;

dark night a bright day sends off, then leaves for

another.

Don't rush off; kiss, raise dust of who the way knew:

on poetry's path a thousand like you have been a

traveller!

A brighter star should in this world light my

destiny...

a flowering fate should push ripe wisdom in

me!

In flagons from far away wine I can't stand to bring;

lane where who supply wine my house must

be!

False are friends, to meet painful; if real, bitter is

parting…

my eyes hurt as they don't want at friends to be

looking!

That heavy trust the sky couldn't carry Adam lifted:

wine the cup could not hold, into dust God was

pouring!

No complaint You offer, immune to all flirting

are You...

Master, tell, You're whose friend, who loving

are You?

With Your radiance creation spills over, but where's

who can drink Your wine, for powers testing

are You?

No sparks were rising, not a bit of ash survived

the burning…

I burnt up, but still don't know what manifested

the burning!

In the day I need a lamp to light my house it's so dark:

with lack of lustre of shining sun my heart fed…

the burning!

Winebringer, a glance, so that I can which cup it was

recognize

I drank wine from that chains of my reserve open did

prise!

I'm a ship waves wrecked and destruction's my destiny:

from the water I've been pulled to be tossed into the

fires!

Indifferent is love and us it has destroyed...

so what;

ship's smashed by that ocean over our head:

so what?

With us in-between the seven skies go on turning:

Ghalib, of our fate don't ask, if soon dead,

so what?

That with Your sword You will my heart part,

swear!

Arrow's wound is not it, I need more, heart is

sore!

If you're a man don't seek comfort on this journey:

pull from feet thorns, with cloak they tangle

more!

O if only heart wasn't pierced by all seen before

me...

I could have passed day constantly travelling...

comfortably.

For bright fire of my lament the spark is no match,

it leaps out from the stone but mine enters it...

piercingly!

They said… 'One should never any wine be

drinking!'

It was in a worthy cause untruth they were

telling!

With effort you reign, but it's with ease I submit:

of you they're talking and of me also they're

talking!

In living, breathing life a dead heart joy is feeling:

how?

Joy of morning's breeze a plucked rose is feeling...

how?

What use are eyes to you unless they can see danger?

Unless dagger pierces heart, any joy it is feeling?

How?

Qit'as...

They, took beak of nightingale and a wing of a moth
and ground them into a mixture and made my being.
For You heart and soul I sacrifice, but ask not how...
one whose taste is to pluck roses, knows gardening?
I take pride in joy of intoxication that has defeated
the worry of the disaster of death suddenly arriving.

Fire... are the lute and the cup and the tune and the

wine:

from fire-eating salamander pleasure-feast of mine

discover.

Free from the taste of your cruelty is impossible to

exist...

what is touchstone for my causeless complaining,

discover.

Winebringer, the wine you pour out, drop by drop,

causes

these lips of mine to laugh at desire for Paradise's

river!

In surrender's compassionate winehouse we were

raised…

at Your feet pride's head, held high… is now laid

down.

The fame of our Friend can be seen in our mirror of

astonishment:

our breath that is lost is way to Friend's street of

renown.

In the rose-garden each pathway leading to Your

sight

is in our desire's openness a tear in which I could

drown.

By sorcery of thought is glorious creation I am

awestruck:

do not go and hold up any mirror... before this

one.

To addiction of pleasure in this world, do not

succumb...

on candy let our fly alight and not any honey-

bun.

About how long is love's journey do not me be

asking...

on road camel-bell's ring is like dust falling on

everyone!

Like rose-bud, your pure body's erotic

fermentation

burst, tore your delicate body's skirt's

tightness!

From madness we drew image of your

flirting...

we painted your playful, loving way in

colourfulness!

Your blazing beauty's heat your veil burns away:

it is obvious veil's obstruction it isn't preferring!

Of wine I'm proud when reflecting your beauty:

it is as though, sun into cup one was squeezing!

The wine began boiling from heat of your desire:

you pour wine from clear flask into cup, playing!

Good news for my heart of my friend coming

secretly:

through claiming piety, I that one have now

deceived.

Wine and the beloved so fascinates the world

one

could think that after Adam to earth Heaven

descended!

Ghalib, perfection's goal is still a long way...

away:

poetic skill isn't enough; test with heavy bow

extended!

If you want to offer justice after cruelty, to me

it's not unusual…

if you won't reveal face to us, out of timidity,

it's not unusual.

You are playful and I think your nature is so good:

but, if through anger love becomes love, truly

it's not unusual.

I am involved with a singer who is like a Venus...

so if my lips go on singing out some melody,

it's not unusual!

Gone are wine and beloved but with my poetry I'm

happy…

in the garden that is now bare a willow tree I have

planted.

A sorrowful angel's Ghalib who by being drunk on

proximity

divine revelation has delivered in the *ghazals* he's

created.

To each other confusion grief and joy bring:

day's light came to farewell dark of night...

then left.

A full portrait lightning wanted to show,

but merely held a mirror to Your might...

then left!

Thinking of you lovingly stopped my tears,

this heart is a fire where smoke is rising

no more.

My complaints of injustice you don't hear:

ah no, all hopes I had I am now having...

no more.

I could lie to heart of your promise of grief;

but, our pride in you're the truth telling:

no more!

To others heart reveals its splendid gifts...

pity it had for all who it were envying:

no more!

To the path's thief heart gave its richness

grieving for you; loss and profit taking:

no more!

You're in my dream, drunk, blouse open wide:

I've no idea of spell my passion's casting

tonight!

"Your curls are in whose hand?" Heart cries!

The chains of Majnun who is shaking...

tonight?

Ghalib, separation's pain is long, so be brief:

on Last Day tell what you're not telling

tonight!

Sparks didn't fly up and no ash is remaining,

I'm burnt but don't know in what way

I'm burnt!

For me hell is unfit as I'm an infidel of love:

by the zeal due to Sanaan's life, today

I'm burnt.*

Don't think desiring you I leapt into fire...

from pain in heart that does disobey,

I'm burnt.

Sanaan (d. 1159 A.D.) was a Shaikh who had over four hundred followers. He fell in love with a Christian girl and supposedly left the path of Islam. Some of his followers went to a Perfect Master and asked for advice, for Sanaan had given all his money to her and had pawned his religious garment to buy her the wine that she wanted. Finally for her sake, he started looking after pigs. The Perfect Master rebuked Sanaan's disciples for not having enough faith in their leader and sent them back with advice on how to bring him back to God through prayer. This happened, and the girl became Sanaan's disciple, for he was now a Master, having experienced that which it was necessary for him to experience to gain God. See Farid ud-Din Attar's 'Conference of the Birds' English translation by C.S. Nott p.p. 34-44 pub. Shambhala

With what hope can heart be chained like this?

My desire's now a screen between you and me!

When your reflection in the mirror flatters you,

think of what our heart feels if you it does see.

That gossip's not from here, why be kind to that one?

One's grief cannot be explained completely...

that's the truth!

You toss away your veil, then I am accused by you!

All I said: "In rose-garden rose fascinates me,"

that's the truth!

Like when one's drunk from heart the secret slips,

with gentle breeze your fragrance in spring

comes.

From theft of pain you give I'm proud of my profit:

I breathe and sigh that its mark's reaching

comes.

With plectrum's help I will not tell heart's secret:

if lover's instrument breaks, cry repeating

comes!

That one wine is giving to all invited to the party,

but when it is my turn, that one is spilling

the wine!

My mouth is watering from joy of wine's taste...

from my mouth pours what I'm not having:

the wine!

Heart, do not grieve if the job is difficult:

when it is beyond doing, it becomes easy.

But in my poetry where's infidelity, faith?

My poetry is in faith, and is in infidelity!

On the Final Day when all are asked of their works,

O if only God would ask us about our desires

unfulfilled.

You told me, I should not be wanting to see You...

but, it's a sin I will do, even on that Day all is

fulfilled!

I can see in Your cruelty my destination…

if in my lap are roses, I'm trembling

for the rose-garden.

When, of Your scent and colour I boast…

my heart's Yours, even if I'm longing

for the rose-garden.

For both of us it was so fine, that fortune did
give me elegant words... you a beautiful face!
From mosque to tavern winebringer took me:
a few cups... then flagon put me in my place!

When no news arrives of garden's prisoners,

my nest is shaken by the net's gathering up.

O Ghalib, I have been faking this madness:

it'd be fine if Friend my trial was taking up!

Heart melted from the weeping and furthermore

with the useless hope of a result getting,

what to do?

We can't in envy of self begin to think of others:

with Khizer in this pathway of loving...

what to do?

Let one drink if one wants to get drunk on wine:

preacher, God help you; with preaching

what to do?

In paradise's garden ask for wine, don't be contented:

whatever the Friend took, now that One will be

giving in return.

To madness give wealth that is gained by wisdom...

Generous One for a gain, thousand losses is He,

giving in return.

This eloquence of ours is not worthless for that One

so Kind our heart takes, and this tongue is to me

giving in return.

God for each act of faith gives a new oppression...

O Ghalib, witness how that Friend is obviously

giving in return.

I'm proud of that beauty whose fame makes it glorious:

it put fear in rose's heart and confused the light

of the candle.

Without help from spark, smoke, flame, I melt breath:

from an inner scar I burn, that's unknown to art

of the candle.

If house has a lamp there is no madness there:

if the heart's in dark of some dusty corner

why be afraid?

Through my being that fool, lightning struck:

if of that fiery breath one has no real fear,

why be afraid?

If you agree with me, time no power wields...

be constant, then about sky's cruel finger,

why be afraid?

If drunk, suddenly from gate of rosegarden you come,

by itself the rose will grow to the edge of our turban.

We want to be alone, busy in reputation guarding...

essence of our walk is dignity, a kind of intoxication.

An edge to our words comes from grief heart bears...

in our mirror the parrot for us, then verdigris became.

We drank the morning cup by melting down our self:

doomsday's morning sun is our goblet... all the same.

With our faith we are not pleased, or of your cruelty:

ah no, the lack of success of your trying to me maim!

Stop this flirtation, of heart and soul take psssession:

my tenderness can't stand all your constant playing.

I'm a mirage of fire from dejection, candle in a mirror:

for sake of onlookers the lie of gallanry I'm practising.

We drew a line through world's existence, eyes closed:

we left ourself and the world with us we were carrying.

You don't worry prey is restless in indifference's trap...

I don't know what stopped a careless way of glancing.

Friendship flows from distance: O you are so bashful

under the veil's cover, you... infamous us are making!

Ghalib, of the cold beware in breast of self-satisfied...

obligations on heart of the impatient, beyond counting.

One's heart is from You, existing due to Your desire

to buy it... all my talk of profit and loss is due to this.

There are streams of wine and and honey in paradise,

but the one and the other for me You ruby lips this is.

As the one born of a fairy they're trapping in a bottle,

so in my heart Your lovely face I hide from other eyes.

Through heat of my walk many thorns are set on fire:

obligated to me are travellers footsteps, believe this!

Ghalib, I'm a traveller on fire who into river plunged:

my only sign are my provisions on the bank... this is.

The fire rises and amazed all of the people stare:

in this great commotion let me reveal my talent.

Last Day, They'll check heads for prayer-marks:

head's scars from madness for you I will present!

I have no other reason from heart's contentment

but to draw a couple of breaths... much afflicted.

Usefulness of Ghalib's eloquence I will explain:

from vein of speech, liver's blood I've extracted.

Ocean's bubbles shows my blistered feet seeking You:

O You light of my eyes, O You jewel so rare…

where are You?

Of perfume and dew of rose our old hut isn't worthy:

O torrential flood and violent wind… where,

where are You?

In these sighs of mine I cannot taste any salty tears:

O light of eyes that don't sleep, just stare…

where are You?

There's much worry, caused by notes in my breath…

O invisible plectrum's pluck beyond compare

where are You?

Last night, on your bed and pillow, no roses...

where is rose's thorn, your soft body pricked?

You: "Your heart's torn, if leaving my lane!"

Where is heart but by cries, isn't comforted?

Don't ask me about *rends* lackadaisical ways,

all I know is that it's not so easy to live easily.

Giving up being with others, is pleasurable...

like Khizer from most people hidden try to be.

I am grabbing a kiss, then, I say that I'm sorry...

so, into etiquette's rules I add a new something!

From evil eye you be shielded; as I've thought to

receive favour, what foe does is a friendly thing!

Divine Mercy's scattering of roses I recognized:

so, at those dry acts of obedience I am laughing!

I flap my wings, but to be free I am not anxious:

I'm bird of longing, but I'm in net of expectancy!

In sea are waves, from it is no knowledge of self:

I am also helpless when I have to break from me!

A ship with no master, my adventures don't ask:

only by smashing myself, on seashore I now be!

I remember that time your respect I enjoyed…

my sighs scattering fires, eyes tears shedding!

From that flirtatious infidel I expected glory:

even in union longing's rush is, what giving?

One's form is bent when much of life's gone:

this reveals that upon me a burden, is laying.

My thought's real nature wanted heart to bleed:

on beauty given me by God on the cheek I'm red!

From spring passed, I learn of colour and scent...

grieving: I tricked my heart, in my life, afflicted!

I trick my heart with tyranny, from your favour:

I'm so simple that in your trap I'm one trapped!

Thoughts are upheavals from beginning to end…

lightning every moment, one seems to be

facing.

Scar on my privacy's brow is candle's black face:

on gathering's carpet my harp's silence is

humiliating.

My disciple was Majnun in the art of madness:

jewels from her camel on you Layla kept

scattering.

That we may think about it is not enough,

you tell me in love the sigh to hear

is the way.

I wish to kiss your lips, then life give up...

in love one must know lack of fear

is the way.

To get to the *Kaaba* why go from temple

to it? Go with face turned to rear

is the way.

Ghalib, drink heart's blood in this world;

to gain wine, to be rich my dear,

is the way!

I am a morsel of roast *kebab*, of wine a wave...

see my turmoil, then of my burning desire

ask me.

Strength to open wings is not from sleeping...

Adam is from Nothing, of his endeavour,

ask me.

I made Paradise, from me seek Kausar's joy...

of Zam-Zam's taste as I'm *Kaaba's* cover,

ask me. *

*Notes: Kausar or Kauther is a fount in Paradise. Zam-Zam is the sacred well
at Mecca. The Kaaba is the sacred site in Mecca, a cube covered by a black cloth.

You enquired about our health from another, thanks...

this reveals at least, that you didn't know our

state!

Thank you freedom, that joy, grief, in heart don't stay:

pure blood and wine are same in our sieve, to

grate!

Ghalib's life, why think this one to talk has power?

You are cruel to ask us about our state, it is...

unfortunate!

Manifest or not, to thieving grief it's dedicated...

heart flew from breast like colour from face

is!

How to lose identity in love is worth the sight...

in our mirror Your reflection taking our face

is!

Ghalib, from my eyes tonight all of it must drip:

maybe heart's blood last night wine of grace,

is.

Over turbulence of my nature I've no control...

my pearl's lustrous waves made me one

impassioned!

Like waves in pearl's lustre I'm concentrated...

but still heart wings that flutter freely

desired.

To a sense of honour I'd give life at seashore

if a tidal wave any frown for me bore, I

suspected!

I remember at love's end I gave heart to heartstealer

who made to me the promise to be faithful…

completely!

To keep secret I've no strength, yet I fear disgrace:

maybe in silence I seek who knows my tongue

adequately?

In human composition the first is heart's anguish:

smeared with blood is root of all hair in all of

humanity!

I'm freed of all anxiety by heart's restlessness:

one can find peace in the rocking of this

cradle.

Your nature is obvious by the fire in that face:

deceive my eyes how long with wine's

ladle?

Winebringer's bright face in the crowd seeing,

before my eyes like a drunken rose set

candle!

As you from that rival's side come, on your way I die:

despairing at your open flirting heart I might

recover!

All those veils that cover your face in desire's heat...

are as a curtain in instrument that's for you to

discover!

Leave the mirror so I'm not by reflection deceived,

I am seeing the vision of the reality of unity

tonight!

I've opened stream of blood from each hair's root...

with red glow of sunset bed I decorate newly

tonight!

Though I failed to find mouth I'm proud of words:

subtle distinction between real and illusory,

tonight!

It's long since joy's law from my mind was wiped:

what before I learnt, that lesson I'll set free

tonight!

Your sweet lips are the very essence, soul

of salt...

and what I say is with tongue, from hole

of salt!

Your generosity and wrath are kinds of flirtation:

in Your time flirtation is a mine, whole

of salt!

O Ghalib, these words of mine, are my wealth...

salt is itself the jewel in the mine, goal

of salt!

I've a heart of a nature touchier than a blister;

gently I place foot, for thorn's tip is also

delicate!

They fall to pieces in the wafting of a breeze:

like rose's petals for us door, wall are so

delicate!

Eyebrow was so upset that it turned away...

we're hard of soul but affliction's, O no,

delicate!

A strange state: a promise, also favour's denial...

it's not our life but the wine that twice can be

given!

One can't be still between glory and the calamity:

for one thirsty to see You, paradise is a mirage

unproven!

One that last night sucked sweet lips drunkenly

is content today to not take cup, even if from

heaven!

I'm happy that the pain in heart a sadness casts

on the marrow of patience; it eternal bliss is

creating!

Of the passion we have it's best to be envious…

I'm happy my heart never again for union is

hoping.

From the ill-fated times all lost desires we take

are to bottom of hope's cup dregs that go on

clinging!

In middle of God's creatures seek the one God:

world's mirrors for a new seeker is school for

uniting!

Where I sit on ground among my *ghazal's* melody,

dust should have rose's scent and musk fill air

fragrantly!

Either beyond paradise my desire shouldn't aspire

or a real refuge for hope I should have found…

secretly.

So those beggars may not borrow conceit's show,

cost of display of speech raised higher should

be!

You came to me privately, but from pride gave no kiss!

You then went to the party and took payment for

singing!

Your scent intoxicates the nightingale that faces rose:

vainly bashful before gardener, rose's forehead is

perspiring!

I thought the burden of grief would go by writing note:

when to wing of bird I tied it, that pigeon was...

palpitating!

The dust of the way we throw on our bare heads

for one with a lopsided turban roses seeking

is!

Apart from any ceremony, a bit of hopefulness am I:

despite indifference that one my grief pitying

is!

Look at sweat on fiery cheek when that one is silent:

tumult of those words beyond exaggerating

is!

Don't talk of any hearing or talk of secret of words:

in painter's brush images, music in a string

is!

If You're moved by pity, fulfil Your lovers wishes:

or, by us giving in, fate's power shouldn't

be weighed.

Our aim isn't fulfilled, don't ask of joy of journey:

blind are eyes; our unsellable goods can't

be weighed!

Heart's agitated, stirring with delight each moment

for behind vine's tendril even without breeze is

swaying.

In blood I drown from envy but from delight I dance

when in the hand of Farhad I see that axe begin

moving. *

O Ghalib, the breath of Jesus your pen it does reveal

when in that way that God has given it begins

writing. *

Witness envy in faith's pride where claims are made!

Witness how without control they rush to goal

anew!

Beneath knife of the father the son places the throat

while the trial of Nimrod's fire the father goes

through!*

*Note: Nimrod built a great fire and threw Abraham into it. God turned it
into a bed of roses. Nimrod built the tower of Babel.

I'm happy I'm off to the *Kaaba* without provisions,

as travelling light mimosa thorns my feet don't

curtail!

I'm a poet, writer, sinner, fine companion, skilful:

even so, I see you have no mercy as I weep and

wail!

Ghalib has no wine, but if seen drunk at dawn on

road know not from own bed that one left that

trail!

Words not from the heart can have any effect?

Any tongue, let it be cut, that no blood is

shedding!

Winbringer is wise, wine is strong, but I was

angry as I thought cup wasn't heavy when

carrying!

I forget myself but want time to find my Self:

I need then no one but thought of Friend...

caring!

My stifled desires and lustful expectations

are greater when I hear grief isn't always

staying.

The mind I asked: 'Sign of a wise one, what is

it?'

It answered: 'Whose words with actions does

fit!'

Heart's scar scattered flames even in old age:

though night ends, this candle is not yet

extinguished!

Day They hid power in wine and cry in flute,

no thought to the work of the mind They

pondered!

And if They've made scar and increased pain

I'm proud in all this tumult, They me...

remembered!

Why ask from what seed these scars are growing?

Take heart from my chest to tulip-planters

please!

You hate your flattery so leave the heavy of soul:

ask who'll surrender soul, from restless take

peace!

God, by madness laid grief's foundation in my mind:

from wall and door's mould many wastelands

make!

Those lightning flashes that the scenery are melting,

let it go and in my vision's cup of joy it to pour

take!

Pleasure of affliction that poor person doesn't know:

in path of my giver of cures me a thorn there…

make!

Opportunity went, stifled desires feet firmly stuck:

I am beyond cure and yet no one's spell binds

me!

Lovers anger me that to Friend attribute my state:

to kindness of the sky none has ascribed this

tyranny!

Ashamed of our heart we still ask killer a favour:

when no other can do it how can we cure self

permanently?

In the learned and devoted one shouldn't trust:

one talks through vanity, the other chases

futility!

From a drunken beauty don't take an easy kiss:

don't buy from a wineseller what is bought

cheaply!

God's only known by feeling, world by mind...

Ghalib, this chant's cry wants to be heard,

loudly!

Any happening of indifference with the lover

reveal to complain is shameful, by death

punishable!

If with Khizer I don't go it's I feel unworthy:

I'm afraid he'd die for as companion I'd be

terrible!

A rare delight is anguish, when it's relished

lover secretly gains pleasure while openly

perishable!

*Notes: Khizer is often called: "The Green One" for he was said to have drunk from the Fountain of Immortality and gained Eternal life. He has been identified with Elias, St. George, Phineas, the Angel Gabriel, the companion of Mohammed on a journey which is told in the Koran, viii, 59-81, and throughout the literature of Mysticism has appeared to many great seekers who eventually became Masters. See my 'Khidr in Sufi Poetry' New Humanity Books, 2012.

I don't talk of foe, grief given... hard to swallow:

scars from unjust cruelty, from friends I've

received!

How to caress you tight enough to my breast?

Before I've often to you about tight blouse

complained!

Heart's joy the veil of success will finally open...
that I get that from grief over You, brings me
happiness!
In Your reign at time of sight, rose is ashamed...
in still blood, scene and rose are drowned, a
mess!

My nest was destroyed, but... heart loves ruins:
with grief's prisoners, walls, doors do not agree.
Be not proud, devotee, you broke my holy thread:
none from my forehead, steals bow to idol of me!
Ghalib, any tear stays unshed due to my crying:
flood did arrive, washed from eyes ability to see!

Don't wish us drunks be lost due to Your pride's graceful

gestures...

to such ones as us the fresh, free breath of the new spring

come.

You cut Yourself off from us and Yourself to others pledged...

but, as promise of to us Your faithfulness isn't binding,

come!

There are different tastes to meeting and parting from You...

If You go a thousand times, hundred thousand returning,

come!

By your flirting I have been tricked, and so, I wish that none

to make enquiries about my soul that with hope is filling

come.

Than Your nature the nature of patience is even much finer:

through lack of use heart and hand numb are becoming:

come!

To affirm existence in a monastery isn't thought unusual...

don't go! Winehouse sells intoxication, so there going,

come.

Ghalib, if you are wanting to your security make stronger...

then like us into circle of humble drunkards, drinking,

come!

That wine I'm desiring that when poured

makes flagon circulate due to its ferment.

Winehouse owner stay calm, I'm innocent:

when drunk to wear pilgrim's cloak I went!

So none falls into trap who loves the form,

to bait the snare I wish no grain was spent.

As in Invisible is my faith, from Friend's

invisible mouth I want to be more content.

There is usually much trouble for the few:

each moment for others delight is evident!

Heart-stealer's mad, Ghalib, no kiss ask,

although love says same is every moment!

They are all fire: my cup, my wine and my poetry;

through the salamander, find way to my pleasure.

Without the pleasure of pain life is hard to live...

touchstone of my grief without cause... discover.

You pour water of fire from flask, drop by drop...

my lips start to laugh at need for heavenly water.

I cannot stop the turmoil in my inner self raging:

a tempest's raised by what's in the pearl's centre!

The raging soul though held like waves in a pearl,

as heart's overflowing with longing to go higher.

To save honour I will die of thirst at river's shore

if I see at the forehead of the tide a frown it cover.

To stop being is the conceit of being a single drop:

when turned into ocean, pride we give up, forever.

Beloved's beauty by own reflection is captured...

joys of such closeness, failing sight will uncover!

Many wayfarers tire in the valley of imagination:

Your desire enchants vigour of limbs of a dreamer.

Our despair has, (not like days), no revolution...

day that was dark once, no dusk or dawn knows.

Beloved's lips I kiss, but to bite them don't dare;

I've a weak heart, no courage to act, take blows!

Dancing in air for You is each mote of my being:

no end is found in madness of desire, that grows.

I'll not dread a thing if I consign self to disaster;

pain of imprisonment, a caged bird never knows!

See nightingale in garden and moth as company;

their longing is such, each no composure shows.

According to one's desire each drop is given out;

in grace's winehouse, no cup or flask that glows!

Words not coming from depth, are worth what?

Tongue no blood shedding, be cut off, by blows!

I travelled out from my self, as I needed to rest:

I wish to return and to only Friend that knows!

Hope of one longing and being rejected are hot,

due to the joyful news that grief... finally goes!

At the method of grace with its longing I'm exalted,

the candle and lamp to the desert's dark night

is spring.

The rules of Your nature understanding is autumn...

that beauty of Your face's mirror, outright...

is spring!

Desiring You my madness is rough of mind's face;

way to You comb of curls of dust of delight,

is spring

Garden is border of carpet, companion of Yours...

for martyrs of Yours, candle at tomb's site,

is spring!

To Your fragrant curls the breeze adds ambergris:

busy applying rough to Your face so white,

is spring.

In dust of fluttering wings of colour wilderness is:

prey frightened from hiding place, outright,

is spring!

Due to love is heart of beauty's power in world...

collecting noise from thrush's cry of fright,

is spring!

Why is spring into mountains and wilderness?

Scattering thorns in paths of those uptight,

is spring!

About *houries* of Paradise sage knows nothing:

would deflower but leave still pure! Upright

is spring!

We've a conversation due to my love and your beauty,

as Khusraw with Majnun, Shireen with Layla,

the other!*

I have had a problem since I gave my soul to the world:

on one side disgust with time, love of the drama,

the other!

You, trying to confound my mind in this play of effects,

one side singer with songs, cup and winebringer,

the other.

Those thorn strewers are afraid by my sighs lightning...

on one side those young oafs, the wise old sir,

the other.

On the journey to be dejected, or in wandering, ecstatic;

on one side cash for inn, desert provisions for

the other.

Pulled left and right by heart and mind I'm anguished:

on one hand a hidden pain, a visible disaster

the other!

You holding mirror to look, attentive to what you see,

on yourself have pity, leave pity for this lover

the other.

Ghalib, what help can you give cypress-like beloved?

In one way rival's envy pulls me, but my desire

the other!

Be doomed by gloom will be the light of the lamp

and full of folds house of pleasure's carpet

will be.

In fever of self-destruction like toss of rue-seeds,

all are hot and wish for leaving self, is set:

will be!*

By appearance of glory of self beauty will melt...

from music's veil, making a self-shroud, poet

will be!

In its way world will make indifference its own:

blood that quarrels yours and my precept...

will be!

All veils fall from the face when we work as one:

told to crowd privacy of believers at onset,

will be.

Ghalib seeks a winehouse in depth of each word,

so others by line from my *Divan* drunk get,

will be!

*Note: Rue seed in Iran is burnt to ward off the evil eye and in magic.

I'd be happy for two witnesses to argue on flattery…

creating subtle insight, breath of antimony…

silent!

To put it succinctly, my heart inclines towards piety;

due to devout's ignominy, to state of an infidel I

went!

Ghalib, I don't care I'm with the beggars now classed,

because in the soul's realm as a sovereign I'm

present!

That soul's fortunate that grief entirely seized,

from our grief enquire of joy of expectancy

of ours!

Intoxicated, we're blown like rose's fragrance:

don't ask; smashed is free will constantly,

of ours!

As rose's colours shine, its heat increases too;

one says spring is *kebab* of fire, inwardly,

of ours.

If spring under its skirt had not concealed it...

foes see unveiled the love for You, madly,

of ours!

If in longing, we are happy in our vagrancy...

if grabbing Your skirt's end is fist, dusty,

of ours!

The young candle here grows as it goes down:

Ghalib; melting, waters deepest locality

of ours!

Friend's beauty its own glorious manifestation is loving,

give happy news of eyes nearness that failed to reach

destination.

Through fatigue they're lagging, now in illusion's valley:

longing for You carves a path through sleeping foot's

vein!

For perfection of our own image the destination we are...

Your glorious appearance is hidden in us from lack of

direction.

Ghalib, I've cut me off from all, so that after all of this

I can find a quiet corner and worship that Divine…

manifestation!

Destiny gives all a duty due to a certain measure...

quick-footed have the job of valley of grief

traversing!

If a seeker on the path you must efface your self...

through valley hard to bear is baggage of a

wrongdoing!

In world upper and lower class, proud and humble:

Ghalib; first, ignore; other to their fate be

leaving!

Reflection of body in water in the wave trembled,

this effect has been made even by fear of own

glance.

Heart of nightingale search, in dewdrop it isn't:

close ear to rose that makes these moans by

chance.

We increase ambitions when the capital's less:

whatever from mind comes is a dangerous

dance!

Simple hearted mirror with this vision pretends:

it needs fill its own desire from a drunken

glance!

This made breath fiery, that melts our heart…

than sight our lament's in a more soulful

trance!

Mouth, bud did not envy when it became rose:

by seeing this, from face veil was lifted; a

glance!

Eye became confidant by heart's intoxication:

tearer of veil, veil-holder became… due to

circumstance!

Freedom of detachment and heart's surrender

inspire Ghalib, who of self is unaware by

happenstance!

I'm proud of that shy glance that hearts ravished

in a away that even those alluring eyes were

unaware.

If drunk, needing help, there are paradise and hell:

who wants Grace, about flame or rose doesn't

care!

Ghalib, don't take your poetry outside of India…

stone and jewel, miracle and trick, are same

here.

When in the water fell reflection of that lovely form,

as if it was a mirror that stream ceased its flowing.

Soul doesn't leave form due to my weak struggling:

my lack of strength's also reason for my not dying.

My back's bent, turning my face towards the past:

in old age how much is found youth's lust, stifling?

By my heart I've been killed but those who oppress

have oppressed us with desire of heart, so lovingly.

You cast a glance on me but with scowl on brow...

such a heavy stirrup but such a light reign holding.

Your face is absorbed by flirtation, in the mirror...

a bewitching eye is door to subtle discriminating!

Anger from the enemy and veil for me is concealed:

fine is heart-stealing, wonderful heart-ravishing!

With empty-handedness what is my life's profit?

our job's to dance, arms in ecstasy, wine drinking!

You, who in this valley gave good news of Huma:

to lover of freedom its shadow on head's hurting. *

From party, taste for poetry brought Ghalib out;

in style of Zuhuri and Saib, self I am absorbing. *

*Notes. The Huma is a bird symbol for God in the beyond state.
Zuhuri (d. 1616) & Saib (d. 1676) are two poets of the elaborate so-called 'Indian
Style' of Persian poetry who influenced Ghalib. See my 'Sabk-e-Hindi' The
Indian Style in Persian Poetry' New Humanity Books 2016.

The wave's strength is from the sea's boiling rage;

sword's thirst by sacrifice's blood flowing is

quenched!

One can't fulfil heart's desire despite being near,

us thirsting on brink of stream in the mire is

entrenched!

Reason is blinded by affirmation of God's unity:

nothing exists but God, all else is illusion,

wasted!

Really, we're self's essence but due to delusion of

duality between Self and Ghalib, obstacles

existed!

In flights of spring clouds how wonderful is the grace

that manifested on earth is what is in heart of the

wind!

Melting of breath in desire for vision of that form…

on sweat on graceful face of Beloved is seen to be

lined.

Touchstone of ancients is in our minds manifested:

wine's purity is seen by dregs in flask's bottom

confined!

You'll have heard how Abraham through fire passed:

see me, without sparks or flames I am totally

burnt!

Cheap to hold touchstone to sight of such flirting...

thousand times I'm testing, I am you can see,

burnt!

I was put in doubt today by the blossoming rose...

maybe on rose-bush branch nest is suddenly,

burnt!

Against the rose-seller in bazaar I can't complain:

but, due to heat of gardener's walk I'm badly

burnt!

You've come, it matters? Fresh from meeting rival!

Heart's complaints, tongue's slander, me...

burnt!

I'm proud of soul melted by desire but what candles

are that by door-curtain of speech... clearly

burnt?

Your coming's good news behind back envy made;

by mirth of roses in garden I'm laughingly

burnt!

Your life is all beauty, my being all passionate love...

by ill-luck of foe, good-luck of friend, it's true I

swear!

You should hold me dear, not for my sake, for Yours:

Master's excellence is proven by slave's good

behaviour!

Not that Ghalib from the worldly expects sincerity:

but if asked about me I hope reply is, 'Alive, in

favour!'

I said, 'Who'll I ask for news of a life that's passed?'

Winebringer then poured in my glass wine of ten

years.

Without a glance those drunken, fascinating eyes...

shed my blood, by that outer corner of one of the

eyes!

Winebringer adorning beauty given by Almighty,

in that garden roses and in Bengal sugar-candy

scatters!

Winebringer's swaying walk liken not to wine...

as it stole lustre from essence of fast-flowing

waters!

How gross you are to cry about pain of separation!

You don't know under the curtain your partner

is Who?

Heart, your key to peace is grief, create an uproar!

If you do not melt from this, to knot decipher

is Who?

You will not buy praises nor sell any complaints!

Heart, you are whose friend, and your master

is… who?

I'm the guardian of my time, I'm waiting for you:

by the repeats of your promises the deceiver…

is who?

I don't know the meaning of 'Who is your God?'

Instead ask me, 'Ghalib, your Beloved, Lover

is Who?'

In restlessness of breeze I tremble in Your street,

I am hopeful perfume will waft from garment

of Who?

Your favour after hearing me is due to my need:

my deep longing comes from infinite torment

of... Who?

I admit I brought the ways of love to the world:

but ignoring justice, introducing discontent,

is Who?

Your fine company is upon lawn of rosegarden:

dispersal of dawn's breeze, its malcontent,

is Who?

My private thoughts the way for prayer did open,

but due to soul's narrow carpet, in throat stuck

prayer.

That one is such a juggler that from me heart was

taken with its thousand of desires that go on...

forever!

Wine is from same jug, fates of drunks... different:

in cup is Jamshid's wine, from gourd dervish is

drinker.

I've made firm faith with help of fear and hope...

in showing of faith mine's hypocritical, a two

facer!

Paradise's porter offered Ghalib milk and honey:

but this poor one from that one, of wine was a

snatcher!

Truly breath of Your kind faith is as much in my

heart as the soul is intermingled with the

body.

God, although I'm the Huma of blessed speech

in this world I've fortune of kite and crow:

measly. *

By tears my breast's on fire, not upon my shirt!

In shirt that unseen thorn at liver pricks,

hurtfully!

It's a pity heart is dead and You don't ask of it:

here it's a custom to enquire of mourners,

sincerely.

*Note: Huma is a bird-symbol for the Beyond State of God.

My desire killed my seeing many roses in garden,

because no room is left and yet Your place

is empty!

Beloved isn't there to see scene, nor lover singing:

rose's place, nightingale's nest, a disgrace;

is empty.

I fill genie in the bottle by agitation of my heart...

of the fascinating air of any speech this face

is empty.

If I'm forbidden to enter mosque by Imam of city,

never by blessing of tavern-keeper my place

is empty!

I am filled by one's side, shoulders, need to hug:

like crescent moon, head to foot, my space...

is... empty!

Listen, spring's breeze wasn't so intoxicated…

it's our dew that the brain is freshening,

the morning's breath!

Effervescence of the wine is our graceful speech

that the wine-cup has aside been casting:

the morning's breath!

In agitation of my being our words so delicate:

You, I am the lamp in Your gathering…

the morning's breath!

Ghalib, when in the morning I took my cup…

roses of thought from garden I was picking!

The morning's breath!

Qasida...

When, pearls of boils on their feet travellers see...

they think beyond height of Paradise their feet be.

They keep in sight, whatever is revealed in eyes...

what is in breast they read from foreheads, easily.

From page of life they all that's right are reading:

on wings of phoenix they the display see clearly!

You of vision of eternity see blindness of cynics:

in this world what they don't see... in other see!

Ask all of vision about Path, that in their speed

they see Way as vein in desert, O so feverishly!

Out of doors in flame that unexpectedly rises...

they think string in stone a pluck strikes easily!

In each drop that into a shining pearl is turning

on face of the river they see blisters appearing!

In brilliance of morning star they see the night,

and in appearance of a bat see daytime's light!

In a magnificent palace they see a wilderness,

in a reed they see Zulaikh's love and loveliness.

And, if they like Majnun are to be wandering,

if they see caravan of Layla, won't be telling!

Drinking own blood, they in teeth hold liver...

if at table alone, they many sweets discover!

As if a knife on their lives is a drop of water,

loaf of bread in throat is like glass, a cutter!

Forehead dot of Hindu is like life's centre…

like the candle in the church is wine so clear.

Wand, dot on forehead, holy thread, all that

are seen as they see cloak, rosary, prayermat.

Not tying souls to form or world of colours,

what they see is seen as show with detours!

They seek cup, in abandon aren't abstinent

even if is seen stars of Moses' white hand!

What's impossible in every way they attain

and all not seen anywhere they see… again.

Those of high-rank are seen by them as other

and one who's low they see as a fellow lover.

All these spectacles of splendour they ignore

as through insight of my poetry they explore.

Let Bahadur Shah, bright as sun, be safe from

evil eye as on dome of sky his flag's flying on.

*Note: Bahadur Shah was the last Mughal Emperor and Ghalib's patron…
he was also a wonderful Sufi poet. See Introduction and my 'Bahadur Shah
Zafar, Sufi Poet & Last Mughal Emperor & His Circle of Poets… Zauq,
Ghalib, Momim, Shefta, Dagh: Selected Poems, New Humanity Books 2018.*

Masnavis...

My breath today with trumpet is in unison

and my silence of secrets is the resurrection.

Writing in flashes, I am the vein of stone...

handful of clay, my writing is a dust-storm.

With uproar of pain my heart is expansive:

without a companion a bubble stirs a sieve.

Praise God, Varanasi from evil eye is saved;

it, blissful paradise, is garden to be sighted!

In the future good folk their lips will open...

with faith glorify city of Varanasi... again!

In this garden, whoever takes last breath...

hasn't to bear difficulties of another death.

This garden they believe is hope's summit,

believing if one dies here they'll be with *It!*

How wonderful, it peace to heart is giving,

filth of the body from souls away washing.

By waters, airs of this place don't be upset,

here all bodies are turned into a pure spirit.

Out of your blissful stupor of sleep come...

to cast a glance at all born of spirits, come!

They're all souls with no forms, watching

because clay and water here is not being.

Like scent of rose, grace… is weightless:

they're pure spirits, forms less than less!

Thorns and weeds are a garden, you say:

its dust is life of that garden… you say!

This large city is one in idols believing…

for those drunk a pilgrimage to be taking!

It's a place of worship for the music-lover:

it is most surely the Mecca of this India!

Flash of Sinai is in bodies of the women,

from evil eye by divine light they waken.

There bodies are slight but hearts strong,

seeking wisely, they to innocence belong.

It's their nature for smiles to play on lips

and like the roses of spring, their mouths.

Charms, a garden with glory brimming;

place, a hundred doomsdays conspiring.

Sweetness, than string of pearls, sober:

grace, than the blood of lovers… hotter!

In their tall, slim forms and their gait…

under shade of rose-bush, snare in wait!

They plunder mind with wise flashes…

bud-time of beds… spring of embraces!

By heat of their flashes they kindle fire,

idols of idolaters they priests set on fire!

Gardens of both worlds due to charm...

faces illuminate Ganges... do no harm!

They bring back dead by long eyelashes,

piercing hearts with lances of eyelashes!

Bodies are riches, hearts rejuvenating...

each cap on head, to hearts good tiding.

Due to their drunken beauty waves rest,

through their elegance water learns test.

Their desire seeks the Ganges waters...

arms to embrace spread Ganges waves!

River's restless from heat of their flashes,

becoming water are pearls in the oysters!

Minstrel, strike string with a new kind of plectrum…
adorn my turban with a flower and a new tune strum!
With the flight of that rose-strewing descant I'll tell
all about my heart from my self, pain of heart I'll tell!
Take away this heart ,and from the lyre it out play…
tell through the music from self what you hear today!
The treasure of music be unchaining, then set it free,
and inside that veil find the path that unbeaten be!
With that music of Venus, you be in consonance…
from symphony of mind make songs that enhance.
Because, I understand well that from lips of singer
that such a chant always allures the heart's centre.
Pray for all forms of light with throat and tongue…
for the continuance of life, pray the old and young!
From this dark clay take news to the pearl-seekers,
that like the brilliant jewel it glows, it shimmers!
Moment that nature of the inner, out is flowing,
know, out from each other song a song's flowing.
Even though poetry is a treasure house of jewels,
of its nature mind's intellect is not just for fools.
You know during night as dark as wing of a crow,
you can't find pearl without lamp's light to show.

For beautification of this world, ageing, weary…

if you have eyes for beauty a reason is necessary.

In captivity be opening up the chains of reason,

and I wish each head was not empty of reason!

Reason is the inexhaustible fountain of living:

reason obtains its youth with life… advancing.

Of all those who now live reason is the dawn,

to the night of the Greeks is lamp of Reason.

Before anything else began reason did appear,

it was reason from nature removed all darker.

The sacred Light with measure of God's eyes

in elements appeared, destined… in disguise!

As the sun shines let every atom be shining,

with joy of success… all eyes be overflowing.

You see me as a day of darkness…although

with light heart's core the depth does know!

From source of light this bit of dust shines,

as sands of desert with bright stars shines!

Anyone who all this luminosity is showing

greatness of Reason in essence is praising.

If one behind this veil this truth does know,

as a person of intellect this one does know!

Even if it meant death I'd seek knowledge,

wealth and strength in life... is knowledge!

Door of a pearl knowledge knows to open

and in kernel of poetry treasure does open.

From choked music knowledge veil takes,

from a withheld sound it the magic makes.

You to have a life knowledge is helping...

then pen's movements you're evaluating!

That one drunk upon this wine's vintage

to others gives prize, to their advantage.

Reason, it is its own guide in its ecstasy;

even if it strays it is at home completely.

Winebringer chose path of self-revelation

then the rapture gained was own station.

One drunk on reason is one more awake,

one with much reason wealth will make.

A song coming from soul heart is called,

all drunk to dregs to company is called!

If in company of such drinkers you sit...

as does flute a pen will make music, it!

Known to everyone is delight of poetry...

in this world, with all, life is a guarantee!

As a cure wonderful is meaning of poetry,

an eternal life itself has the best of poetry.

Poetry I discovered is a real friend of mine

for from inner self it seeks reality of mine!

Even if it is a connoisseur of gems, poetry

does combine gems and jewels... equally.

Poetry is the wine and the effect is reason;

poetry is essence, silent tongue the stone.

Your ears measure the worth of the wine,

winebringer is knowledge, drinking wine!

Equally drunk are those in this company,

like scent they together are sent, finally.

In special group all special vests wearing

like a whirling wheel inside... are dancing.

New revelations to self knowledge makes;

from eyes of past... heart, new light takes!

With this treasure in the wild, discerning

ones find in the world a new way of living.

In this circle the ignorant seek their light

from the beggars bearing faces full of dirt.

The title of understanding reason prepares...

in any work of learning, appreciation guides.

Advancement of knowledge is lustre of God

and due to stupidity is no knowledge of God.

The face of all of those learned is awareness

and action of the strong one should harness.

The Sufi finds insights through meditation,

ambition is effect of one's conscious action.

Authority of reason weakens lust, anger...

as if obeyed by wolves and boars, its order.

Giving courage's delight to anger is reason

teaching more patience and lust to restrain.

Engaged in strife reason tactfully does stay

and as wine enjoying abstinent does stay!

From dread of death reason us does save...

and water of life us by thought does it offer.

The habit of decency all our desires require

and the elixir of life our eyes see in the mire.

By knowledge God manifested to laws give

so that we also attain status so we can give.

To let the life flow dissolve in blood the liver

then through immortality of life be the giver.

You know that once one set out horse riding

for wilderness that one set out for hunting...

that one was by magical hound accompanied:

it was hound's magic making one interested.

If that one of interest was increasing speed...

in method of job as a dog was faster, indeed.

Horse like a young, fresh steed didn't run...

as to hound in chase it was an obedient one.

Any who is like that steed and hound acting

is sure to take into hand prey that is fleeing.

And so, no art or any job can be easy to gain

as a glimpse of technique is not imagination!

Because of consciousness, pain is my teacher,

my spring's the autumn of one, the unknower.

From the start pain in my nature is ingrained,

it's hell, but mine a paradise to be experienced!

From such a turmoil the magic of music comes:

when moved from itself... it soon, back comes!

From my own self, I with this heart afflicted...

a clamorous strain of poetry I have often said.

In seclusion I am happy of my own company,

I lament my own self with my heart, so weary.

Over my poetry worldly cares have no power:

freedom has no encouragement from another.

Due to its gloom night was devilish looking:

devil-faced was world, due to profit-making!

I arrested the breath of darkness by leaving...
in form of pain, joy of poetry I was receiving!
Darkness of the dreadful night in that closet
by seeking that lamp for my soul, I purged it.
Away from the fluttering moth is that lamp,
away from all houses that exist is that lamp.
Even one trace of oil in it can never be seen...
in it its flame upon itself lamenting has been.
This is the lamp that without any oil is lit...
it is inside me and I'm consumed by its heat!
To illuminate heart, pain from God comes...
star of my day and lamp of night that shines.
It's not right of me to be complaining of pain,
reason complains of me if I complain of pain!
O my pain, you'll always enjoy my blessing:
these lips will hail you, heart will be aching!
Like Ghalib, may heart be happy with pain,
and this treasure of a desert be filled, again.

Made in the USA
Monee, IL
03 October 2021